SIMPLE.

How Kids Help Us Understand God

Amy Clarkson MD

Cover designed by Amy Clarkson MD

.

Amy Clarkson MD
Visit my website at www.amylclarkson.com

Printed in the United States of America

First Printing: January 2019

ISBN-13 978-1-7940-9984-5

To the women who have gathered with me weekly to study and read and discuss all things, from the deeply spiritual to the mundane challenges of life.

CONTENTS

INTRO

One of the things I learned in medical school was that patients appreciate the simplification of complex topics. It did no one any good to rattle off Latin-based words and superior sounding terms. People even have a name for this; Doctor Speak. For example, a Doctor may tell a patient, "Your Chem. 7 showed elevated creatinine, extremely concerning for acute renal failure, so I need to do a workup and full renal panel." Or a Doctor could say, "The blood work we did showed that one of the proteins your kidneys are supposed to filter is higher than normal. We need to find out if your kidneys are just stressed out from an infection or something else minor, or if there is more going on. To do that, we need some more blood drawn to run a few more tests."

While Doctor Speak is more succinct than using everyday language, it usually creates intellectual distance, and sometimes even fear or misunderstanding.

I always found it satisfying when the light bulb of understanding went off in a patient's eyes as we discussed medical things.

In the same way, there is appreciable gratification when tough spiritual concepts can be simplified and grasped. As a doctor, I would pull out analogies from plumbing to try to conceptualize the heart, or computing or electric circuits to describe something in the nervous system. I've used the idea of a drain for the liver and the armed forces for the immune system. These leaps weren't meant to disrespect the sophisticated concepts of the original, merely to communicate and allow greater understanding overall. It's taking something known, to explain the unknown.

It's the same with theology. In an attempt to take the unexplainable and beyond, sometimes I can understand it better with something immediate that I do comprehend.

As a way to conceptualize specific faith topics, I have noticed in discussions with friends or taking part in Bible study that I revert to my role as a parent or as a grown child who was parented. While I do not pretend to comprehend parenting most of the time, it is in front of me daily, and there are plenty of aha moments available for my guidance.

Here's the thing; you may not be a parent, but you were a child at some point and parented by someone. It may have been a sibling, a relative, or friends. It doesn't have to have looked traditional, and it may have been dysfunctional, but everyone can 'go there' when we talk about kids and parents.

So, let's do this. Let's take a look at ways that kids and parents can help us understand God as he relates to us, his children.

"It can scarcely be denied that the supreme goal of all theory is to make the irreducible basic elements as simple and as few as possible without having to surrender the adequate representation of a single datum of experience."

—ALBERT EINSTEIN
From: Philosophy of Science, Vol. 1, No. 2
(April 1934), p. 165.

Chapter 1 **Pain & Suffering**

You've come across them, in fact, you may be one of them; someone who says they have lost their faith. It's an interesting phrase, almost implying that faith is an object that got misplaced. I suppose for some that's just it; faith is piled somewhere under obligations, schedules, or doubt. Others just don't trust religion as an institution, so they have left the church as an organized activity.

Lost faith can also be a big deal, like losing a friend, or a job, or a pet; as in gone, over, or deceased. Or, it may be someone who has left the idea of God behind. To this person, depending on how vital God ever was to them, the loss may at this point be no big deal. Faith to them is a distant memory of childhood or just a season of life.

Regardless of whether the loss of faith is accidental or intentional, there are countless people right this moment on the brink of walking away from their faith. It begs the question, what took place in the past or what is currently happening, that is nudging these individuals away from belief in God? What causes the "loss"?

Don't you think behind many of the stories of loss you find disappointment? The institution of church failed them, or a person identified with faith failed them, or perhaps even God failed them. There are so many heart-breaking narratives along these lines of abandonment that exist. The failures are destructive and confusing. Whether it's the church or a person that instigated the harm, the deeper question I always hear is, "Why would God, who is loving, allow something unloving to happen?" You've heard that, right? Even if not in those words, it's one of the big questions behind the I'm-out-of-here flight from faith.

This question of why is such an old universal question that to help soothe the dissonance, some people have pat answers they like to dole out. Can you think of some you've heard? For instance, "Well, we live in a sinful world. That's why that tornado just obliterated that town."

What?!! Or, "We all have choices, and those choices have consequences, so don't blame God when you get pregnant at 15." Yikes!!

Another one I've heard people say is that "God can't intervene with everything. If He did, we wouldn't have free will." To which, if I were suffering, I would be sure to reply, "Yes, but I'm not asking for him to get involved with everything or everyone, just me!"

The problem with these one-liners is that they aren't satisfying at all. They don't quench the question. They offer up nebulous concepts. The intent may be to offer hope, but one-liners usually end up making us feel worse than before.

We are going to take a look at pain and suffering in the realm of parent and child interactions, but I'm guessing this won't assuage and get rid of the personal damage you or others may have from past or current unhealed hurts. I do, however, believe it can give us a way to at least begin to understand the constructs in which God has chosen to operate.   It's like if you were playing a board game that you didn't know the rules to, but you were losing miserably, your pain would be two-fold: the pain of losing and the pain of not understanding why you were losing. If someone took the time to explain how the game worked, it might not change your annoyance at losing, but at least your loss would make sense.

To take a look at human suffering, let's use an analogy right before us: our homes. When I say home, I mean the place we live, be it an apartment, a condo, a dorm room, etc. Think about the structure itself: the walls, roof, floors, doors. These permanent objects are the framework of our home, just as there is a framework in the larger world that we live in that includes things like habitat, weather, and the laws of nature.

Much of the pain and suffering we experience in the world, is due to the environment we inhabit. To understand this type of pain we can use the place we live as a mini example of the world. The same natural laws at play within the universe are valid for our homes as well. Picture this then, my home and your home are filled with objects. There is furniture, things on the walls, electronics (too many in my case). You may have carpet or wood floors. Do you have animals? Stairs? Toys lying around? I have all of those, which means I also have dirt, dust, and piles in my home. There may be windows which leak in the cold, and even a door you've meant to fix that bursts open at times when a large gust of wind hits. I mention all of these details because it's important to understand that my home is not static. It's always changing. It will change even if my family or I am not there. In fact, left to itself it will decompose, as things continue to move towards chaos and degradation.

This sounds extreme, doesn't it? But I've experienced firsthand what an abandoned structure can become. My husband's uncle had a cabin he stopped using. This wasn't a rustic cabin. It had plumbing and heat and electricity. Ten years of no humans occupying the place and the cabin was condemnable. Water pipes froze and leaked, mice and animals found their way inside. Wood rotted, fungus grew, and nature took over.

Why is this important to understand? It's crucial because natural law is a real thing at work in the environment. My little home is a microcosm of the world we live in, full of objects both inanimate and alive, always changing. As a resident of planet earth, some of the pain that occurs is merely a result of living in an environment that operates under natural law.

To better explain this, let's take a look at some of the pain and suffering my children have experienced as residents of the Clarkson home, which operates under natural law, just like our environment.

There was a time when each of my kids had grown to the misfortunate height of being a half centimeter taller than the underneath of our counters. For years they had whisked around the home oblivious to the surfaces that jutted out of our island or hung slightly over the counters. But overnight it would seem, they suddenly grew enough to graduate from under counter walkers. The transition was brutal. Unaware of the change, they would gallop for a toy or make a bee-line for dinner, and their little head would run smack dab into the counter.

The first few times were always shocking, the pain confusing, their little minds trying to understand where this object came from. Later, there was less shock and more exasperation when they'd forget and re-injure themselves.

For me, as their parent, it was also terrible. I would often see the collision split seconds before it would happen. I would wince and then hear the thud and outburst. Of course, I'd immediately wrap my arms around them in comfort, trying to sooth the sting. I often caught myself trying to gently remind them, "Buddy, you can't fit under there anymore. I'm so sorry! You've got to remember the counter is there!"

Think of all the potential disasters in our homes! They are innumerable. There are stairs to trip down, corners to run into, doors to slam fingers in, outlets to get shocked from, bunk beds to fall out of, walls to jam toes into.

I can tell you it isn't just the kids who have suffered from living in this home. Just yesterday I misjudged a door opening and ran my shoulder into the door frame. I hollered and lamented my mistake.

Guess what I didn't do though? I didn't blame the home builder for my bruised shoulder. I didn't question the design of the home either. I accept that part of living in this house means there will be some moments of pain that are a result of the home itself.

Take the leap with me. The world is much more complicated than my home. There are things at play like weather, the environment, and the natural terrain that are part of planet earth. These are things completely out of our control. My children didn't choose their height, their flexibility, birth order, gender, etc. and yet those things influence how they interact with the structure and objects that occupy our home. In the same way, you didn't choose what state or country you were born in or what era to arrive in. However, that random part of your life, where you live, changes the likelihood of you experiencing hurricanes, earthquakes, droughts, floods, tornadoes, fires, mudslides, or blizzards.

Those natural events are incredibly destructive. People suffer and die in those catastrophes. To think that God is causing those circumstances, is akin to thinking that as a parent I'm generating the pain my kids experience from growing tall enough to run into counters.

Wait, you say, God is all powerful, right? He *could* stop those disasters if he wanted, so by not interfering he's still culpable. To reason this argument out, let's go back to the home analogy and pretend power was granted to me to intervene in supernatural ways. What might that look like in the head trauma counter situation? I suppose I could make it so my kids wouldn't grow past a certain height; that would be a way to intervene to prevent pain. Ah, but the consequences of being 32 inches tall forever, might offer a different kind of pain. I've got it. I could move around the walls, doors, stairs, and counters continually to prevent anyone from hurting themselves. You know what would happen in that situation, right? To stop one child from smacking into the wall by supernaturally moving it, I would inadvertently cause a different child to run into it, or worse, change the home in such a way that new calamities ensued such as a roof collapse or a storm to blow inside.

The point being, if God began to intervene in the natural world to prevent all harm, to what end would that be? Would there be an arbitrary scale of what was an okay discomfort to go through vs. true tragedy? Stopping the flood today may worsen the drought tomorrow. Bringing sun on your wedding day may interfere with the farmer praying desperately for rain for his crops.

I'll tell you what bothers us about this type of pain; it's out of our control. Sometimes what we try to do to combat that icky feeling of things being out of control, is think our worthiness or goodness has something to do with environmental suffering. The Bible is pretty clear on this one. Matthew 5:45 (NIV) says, "He causes his sun to rise on the evil and the good, and sends rain on the righteous and the unrighteous." In other words, that lighting that struck your neighbor's tree, sending a tree limb through your roof and crushing your car, was not because you haven't been to church in a month. It's just an example of the harm we experience as humans from living in the natural world.

The harm that we experience *just because* we are alive and live in a natural habitat also encompasses more than just weather and natural disasters. What other things do we not have control over that *just is?* What about the structure of ourselves? My severe nearsightedness *just is*. I didn't do anything to cause it, and no one else did anything to create it. It's in my genes. My brother inherited high blood pressure. Not too many high school students need medication to prevent heart disease, but he did.

Pain and suffering from the structure of natural laws at play on earth, as well as the structure of the natural laws at play within our bodies, are not God mandated. You might be wondering why then God didn't make things perfect in the beginning. Why not design a perfect environment without natural disasters and a perfect being without disease and handicaps? Oh, He did. The design, Eden, was perfection. It was us who messed things up.

There is another danger in my house beside the home itself, which is the other people living in the space. Let me tell you this is where I spend a majority of my energy as a parent when it comes to injury and harm. Like my kids, the majority of the pain and suffering we experience in our world is due to the other people that inhabit this earth with us.

Just pause for a moment and think of something painful you recently experienced. Was another human involved? I'm going to guess the answer is YES. The pain from other humans has two forms, either inadvertent or deliberate.

I see this with my kids all the time. Inadvertent pain comes when one child leaves a Lego on the floor, and an unsuspecting foot is assaulted by the sharp edges of the plastic as the weight of the child or adult steps on it. Those little blocks can cause me to scream and hop around like my foot has been cut off.

Other times, the harm is well thought out. I've watched a sibling karate-kick another, or release a nerf dart directly into someone's face. I might have chuckled a little when my son convinced his sister to let him try a "death grip" on her, as she should have seen that one coming.

Those are all examples of physical hurt, but emotional harm is just as present. I wish I could say my children think before they speak. More likely than not, I hear words spoken effortlessly that easily tear down, taunt, and sear their siblings' egos. Like with the physical pain, the words that wound my children are at times deliberate and at times inadvertent. At a certain age, when my son would exclaim, "I got to have ice cream at school today!" The sad faces of his siblings surprised him. He didn't realize his declaration would make them feel bad. However, as he has aged, the same statement is often sent as a purposeful zinger intent on stirring up jealousy.

Here's what makes this type of pain much more complicated: even if my kids never spoke to each other (ensuring no accidental or purposeful hurt form words), and even if they didn't actually play together, (limiting the chance of physical pain), they would likely still get hurt just because they all occupy the same house. The structure of birth-order, gender, personality, and abilities sets them up for constant comparisons. There is pain when one child is naturally more gifted on an instrument and another child struggles. There is pain when one gets invited to a party and the others don't. Just sharing space with people who are different than us is a set-up for hurt.

Let's move it out of the realm of childhood and think about our current selves. How much of our hurts can we blame on the action of others? Sometimes it is inadvertent. Someone runs a red light and slams into a car leaving the driver paralyzed. A doctor might assure a patient that there's nothing to worry about, missing a crucial diagnosis and chance to treat. A woman with her 5th pregnancy could excitedly announce how it seems her husband just had to look at her in the right way and she's pregnant, in the company of a friend who's struggled with infertility for years. These are all examples of unintentional physical and emotional pain.

Unfortunately, many times it is deliberate: bullying, abuse, neglect, belittling, prejudice. Humans are capable of using their actions and words to inflict horrific pain on each other.

Then to complicate things, much of the pain we experience from other people is neither inadvertent nor planned, but just because we share space and were created in unique ways. Every time another human gets the job we applied for, beats us in the competition, makes the team instead of us, or goes on the vacation we've always dreamed of, it hurts. Why? Because their success makes us feel unworthy or it feels unfair. Therefore, by merely living on a planet with other people, we are set up for pain, as the world tries to split us into the chosen and not chosen.

Where is God in this type of pain? The affliction we experience based on the actions of others is often still blamed on God. Why didn't He stop the car from slamming into the other? Why didn't He make the doctor get the diagnosis? Why didn't he prevent the woman from bragging about her prolific fertility? The logic goes, if He can intervene, why doesn't He?

To help grasp this, we need to jump back to the parenting relationship. As a parent I technically have the power to stop much of the affliction my kids dish out to each other, but what does intervention look like?

It's easy to envision grabbing my son's arm right before he smacks his brother, holding him back and preventing injury. But, what about the hurtful taunt that came right before the wind up of the arm? Should I block that too? And if it was a sour look that initiated this, should that be prevented? Here's what I've witnessed as a parent, a little banter quickly can turn into a war of words, spewed with such intensity and volume that many times I've worried our neighbors might hear and wonder what apocalypse was at hand. In the same way, a few gentle nudges can slide quickly into full punches and tears in seconds. Thus, to intervene and prevent the big stuff, I would have to intervene in the little things, which means the only real solution is to ask for separation and silence. They can't speak to each other, and they can't be in the same room with one another. That's the only way to make sure they are pain-free from affliction caused by one another.

You see where we are going, right? To completely prevent pain as a parent I would need to enforce constant isolation. Merely coming in contact with one another would have the potential for something to go wrong, so solitary confinement it would be.

Extrapolating that out to God, if we expect him to intervene in the tribulation we experience from others, he would have to keep us separated and silent.

That's extreme, you suggest. Just have Him prevent the big things. I've heard people say, "Why couldn't God have just stopped certain terrible people from being born." Think of some of the ultra-bad guys out there, couldn't he just have prevented their births? But then again, what's the definition of ultra-bad? Someone causing many deaths? Someone causing one death? Someone causing terrible injustice or harm to many? Someone causing terrible injustice or injury to one? Where would he stop intervening and finally allow someone to be born?!?!

Well, you say, let them be born, but let him just interfere with their free will so they won't do the harmful thing. I could do this for my children too if they were programmable robots. If I could program my children with me in charge of every action, I think we could live pain-free together. But then, as a parent, I'd be sacrificing any hope of a relationship with love and gratitude in it, for the ease of behavior and a peaceful environment. The moment I set myself responsible for every action they take, I permanently take away their ability to freely love me.

God could have made us perfect beings without the ability to make bad decisions, and then we would have been robots. However, if we were robots, there would be no chance for a relationship. Not just relationship with God, but with each other. Without the ability to choose to love, there is no such thing as love itself. Not to mention, robots don't have any real emotions. I don't know about you, but a pain-free existence isn't worth the loss of love and relationships to me.

There is one more concept to explore about suffering; ourselves. Some of the pain we experience is due to our own choices.

Believe it or not, my kids have the hardest time with this one. They would rather sulk and stew and point their finger at their sibling for being the cause of pain than to sit with the realization that they are indeed to blame for their hurt. It can be quite comical watching children avoid blame. We were at the airport recently eating a quick bite in-between flights. A half-filled drink sat on an empty chair that my youngest didn't see. He sat down recklessly knocking the cup over on him, the seat, and the floor. The very first words out of his mouth were, "I didn't spill it!" His pants were soaked, he was embarrassed and experiencing pain. He looked around frantically in his hurt trying to find someone or something else responsible, but undoubtedly, he wanted us to know, it wasn't him.

Just like the previous section, the pain that is due to our self-responsibility can be either inadvertent or deliberate. The drink spill of my son was not purposeful. It was an accident from inattention to his surroundings. In the same way, when I see my daughter zipping across the room at top speed in her socks, I cringe inwardly knowing that this will not end well. Sure enough, I'll hear the sound of her slipping and sliding, and finally the injury. It wasn't on purpose, but the set up was there for disaster.

Other times it is calculated. "If I were you, I'd get my homework done before screen time." They ignore that familiar phrase all too often, and the decision to postpone the work morphs into forgetting, which in turn gives rise to panic and tears the next morning on the way to school. My response is not overly sympathetic, as the pain I witness in my child is not only self-inflicted, but something I had explicitly warned against.

Isn't this true of us as well? Can't you think of an example of self-inflicted pain you've caused yourself? When my husband and I jumped into a remodel project early that went over budget I had the kind of pain that makes it hard to breathe, as I saw our bank account drop to just dollars. I was fearful and upset and in emotional distress, but there was no one to blame but myself.

Self-imposed pain isn't always consciously deliberate, meaning it may take time to see the results of poor decisions. If I'm working sixty hours a week and my marriage starts to fail, what seemed like a right decision to work overtime for more money, may be responsible for the marital strain. Many of our choices may be for good reasons but have unintended consequences that still cause self-inflicted pain.

Where does God fit into the idea of self-induced pain? Just think for a moment about what you do with children and then know that God is doing this more perfectly and thoroughly than we are. For me, as a parent, to prevent self-caused pain, I try to offer wisdom and boundaries. I might set a rule about the amount of technology allowed, to ensure less painful consequences from indulgence. Sometimes I offer advice, suggesting that wearing shorts while it's snowing may not be a great idea.

Do I, though, ever intervene and prevent bad choices? Not usually. I'm not sure my kids would ever learn how to make decisions for themselves or be able to understand consequences and actions if I didn't let them experience the pain that comes from unwise choices. I am aiming for independent adults who don't need to call me when they are 30-years-old to ask me what time they should set their alarm in the morning to have time to get to their new job.

Did you notice I wrote I don't *usually* intervene? There are times I pull the parent card and say, "Sorry, you are six-years-old and not watching The Walking Dead." Or, "You will wear this helmet when you attempt skateboarding, no exceptions."

God does this too, I believe. Usually not intervening with our decisions, but at times closing doors as we try to step thru as a way of saying, "Sorry, definitely not this choice." Now, even when I do intervene to try to prevent major catastrophes, can my kids sidestep my absolutes? YES! My son can sneak an iPad and still watch something we've not given a choice to watch. In the same way, can we blast through a door God's trying to close to prevent a significant hurt? Yes!

For a majority of things, though, like a parent, he offers us wisdom and boundaries that are meant to make life easier and then he lets us make our own decisions. The most basic of these limitations are the Ten Commandments, though the Bible is chalked full of advice on living in a way that reduces the chance of self-inflicted consequences. Everything passed on to us is meant to either protect or provide.

If you have some time, read the Ten Commandments found in Exodus chapter 20. See if you can figure out how each commandment is meant to protect us from brokenness and heartache or provide a more whole and fulfilled life.

I still recall learning in medical school that the reason we give newborns a Vitamin K shot after delivery is to prevent bleeding during circumcision. Babies are naturally born with too little Vitamin K, which is crucial in the clotting process. Our bodies do make Vitamin K, but that doesn't start until the 5th day after we are born. Vitamin K helps the liver produce something called prothrombin which does the clotting, so we don't bleed to death. Interestingly, in Genesis Chapter 17 verse 12, God commands Abraham to wait until the 8th day of a newborn male's life to perform circumcision. Guess which one day of a male's life his prothrombin levels are above the normal level, which means the one day he has more than enough material to protect himself from a cut? His eighth day of life, the specific day God told Abraham to perform a procedure known to cause bleeding.

That command is a prime example of something meant to protect us. We did not discover the actual science behind clotting until the 1930's, and yet God the creator, of course, knew how the body worked and declared the law. Abraham was expected to act out of obedience, not knowing the medical reason why God chose the 8th day.

I would bet you can think of other things the Bible instructs us to do or not do, that can save us from future pain if we abide by the wisdom. Here's a quick example. I'm using the Message version for this because this sounds exactly like something I tell my children! Ephesians 4:31 "Make a clean break with all cutting, backbiting, profane talk. Be gentle to one another, sensitive." Such simple wisdom that isn't an arbitrary command, but there to prevent pain with each other.

As a parent, I am aware of the daily potential for my children to experience a hurt of some kind. It may occur just as an occupant of our home, the only fault being that they are in fact alive and happen to reside in this particular place. Other pain may come from accidental or intentional aggression from the other humans in this house. Finally, there is suffering that comes from my children's behavior, meaningful or incidental actions that are ultimately harmful to themselves.

My role, I think, is not unlike what God does with us. I try to give out wisdom and set rules to make existing together in our space less risky for causing suffering. Ultimately, however, I know hurts occur despite the boundaries. In those instances, my natural reaction is to comfort, sooth, and encourage. Their pain also rubs off on me. My heart aches when my kids suffer, just because I love my children.

Interestingly, it wasn't until I felt that bottom dropping sadness of empathy and compassion for my kids when they experienced pain that I was able to get a glimpse of what God must feel like when I am hurting. It doesn't matter the nature of their pain, whether they ran into a wall, were pushed down by a sibling, or ate an entire bag of popcorn. Their pain at that moment makes my heart ache. I gather them to me to acknowledge their hurt. That's half of the healing, just having someone else say, "I see your hurt, and I am so incredibly sorry that happened to you."

Can you hear and know that God says that to you? Maybe you never had someone say that to you, and it's why you are only half-healed. Whatever the hurt is, know that God sees it and is trying to comfort you. Even if you scream, like my son sometimes does in his pain, "It's all your fault!", God can absorb it, and he is saying, "That should not have happened to you, I am so sorry."

We started with a question, how can God exist or be loving, when terrible and ugly things happen to us all the time? Well, as a parent, I exist and consider myself loving, and yet terrible and ugly things happen to my kids in my own home. I hate to say it, but at this stage, I don't think a day goes by that someone doesn't experience some hurt. That fact in no way changes the reality, though, of my love for my children.

I would even go so far as to say that the pain is the proof of my love. It is my profound adoration for them that provides a home of beauty and complexity rather than a sterile non-harmful space. It is my craving for a relationship that allows for their unique differences in personality and my respect for them as individuals that grants them the ability to make choices. It is my unending love and hope for them to mature into whole beings that allows the consequences of their decisions to play out. An empty room of isolation as a house and robotic exactness for family members is not my idea of loving at all.

Perhaps it's the same with God. The hurts and suffering we experience are evidence of how much God loves us, respects our autonomy, and ultimately desires a relationship with us.

Chapter 2 **Trust**

Before I became a parent, I must admit I had a somewhat romanticized view of parenting. I just knew that my instincts would solve any minor unknowns that might come up. Anyone I heard complaining about how hard it was to parent, I assumed were just complainers. How hard could it *really* be? Famous last words, right?

If you are a parent, what are some of the surprises, both good and bad, that caught you off guard? One of the things I envisioned pre-kids, was that I would have little versions of myself who loved me unconditionally and trusted me without question. I was sure there would be grand adventures when I would hold out my hand and say, "come with me," and they would unhesitatingly reach their hand up and follow wherever I took them. I mean, isn't that where the term "Childlike faith" comes from? This little vision I had played right into what I assumed was the type of faith we were to strive for, non-questioning and quick to trust, just like children.

There is a problem with this train of thought; once I became a parent, I discovered a very different reality when it comes to trust and my kids. My kids aren't always quick to trust me, and often their trust comes with lots of questions, hesitations and initial doubt. There's another more significant problem with the concept as well, the term "childlike faith" isn't even in the Bible!

Surely there are one or two of you having a moment of disbelief like I did when I was delving into this subject, that the well-used phrase in churches of having "childlike faith" is not written in the scriptures. Where, then, does this phrase come from?

Jesus mentions children and the Kingdom of God a few times in the New Testament. The first is in Matthew chapter 18 when the disciples are arguing about who the greatest in the Kingdom would be. Jesus points out a child and says they need to humble themselves like children. Later in chapter 19, He says "Let the little children come to me, and do not hinder them! For the kingdom of heaven belongs to such as these." (Matt 19:14 NIV).

In the gospel of Mark and Luke, He references the need to receive the Kingdom of God like a little child. Specifically, Mark 10:15 (NIV) says, "Truly I tell you, anyone who will not receive the Kingdom of God like a little child will never enter it."

I don't see the word faith in those passages. The references to children use the words humble and receive in regard to the Kingdom of God. Let's think about this, how do kids usually receive gifts? In my family, especially when they were young, gifts were objects of great delight and wonder. The anticipation and reception turned into joy and excitement. Most commentators referencing these scriptures would say it is the character traits of surprise and delight mixed with humility that Jesus is referencing when He speaks of children and the kingdom of God.

Since childlike faith isn't an actual command in the Bible, can children even teach us anything about faith and trust? Absolutely. In fact, I think as we examine trust in the context of parents and children, we will find greater understanding of our issues of trusting God.

The very first thing we need to do is realize that trust is both experience and personality driven. Do you know people in your life who are natural risk takers? Think a moment about them, do they seem to trust quickly or are they more skeptical?

When I think about trust and my kids' personalities, the first image that comes to mind is water. I cannot tell you the number of times over the years I have stood in the shallow end of a pool and said to one of my kids, "Go ahead, jump, I'll catch you!" What happened next was often personality driven. My youngest son, who embodies no-fear and is naturally inclined to trust, would jump with no hesitation. My middle child, however, is overly cautious and not trusting. It would take multiple verbal reassurances and promises, and even then, he often would walk away.

Of course, it's not just personality as experiences also factor in. If a child has lived in an environment where someone broke their trust, it will undoubtedly affect their ability to trust in the future. When my middle son was three, we were at a local lake splashing in their swimming area. My son was enjoying the freedom to walk in the thigh-high water without a life jacket. A ski boat zipped by the swimming area, sending several large waves rolling towards the shore. I was far enough away from him that the first wave knocked him under before I could reach him. Guess what? He refused to swim the rest of that entire summer. Even with a life-jacket and our insistence that a life jacket would hold him above water. Even encouraging him to wade in ankle deep water to see that he would enjoy the refreshing play. Even promising to hold his hand and not let go, it was all rebuffed. His experience completely impacted his ability to trust the water that summer.

To make this more complicated, even the perception that experience is related to an outcome can disintegrate trust. My youngest used to love movie theater popcorn. Even when he was too young to capture the plot of specific movies, as long as he had a container of buttery popcorn, he was content. One night after the family had seen a film together, and my youngest had his usual popcorn delight, he woke in the early hours vomiting. Going around the school at the time was a very rough GI flu bug that he came down with. However, in his mind, it was the popcorn that caused the sickness. The perceived connection shattered his trust in popcorn. To this day, he refuses to eat even one morsel.

Have you seen examples like this, either real or perceived, that have caused either you, a child, or someone you know to be slow to trust in that specific area?

It's important to keep in mind, that experience can work both ways. My son who spent an entire summer deathly afraid of swimming is now a powerful swimmer and loves the lake. The following summer, time's passage had eased some of the fear, and he was willing to trust me to try wadding in the shallow area. Soon he agreed to a life-jacket and venturing into deeper water and finally to holding his breath underwater. Once he took the risk and realized that indeed I could be trusted, his hesitation shortened and slowly disappeared. This is how it is for all my kids, the more my promises ring true, the easier it is to trust the next time.

It's the same in our relationship to God. Our personalities and past experiences play a role in how easily or quickly we trust God. Some of us come into the world more trusting; let's not fault people who are the opposite. Usually, more than even personality, it's our past experiences and more precisely how we interpret those experiences that affect our ability to trust God.

Just imagine if you were consistently in an environment where people broke promises, not only would it be hard to trust another human's promises, but what would the promises of God mean to you?

This idea that how easy or difficult it is to have faith in God, or God's word, or even God's church, based on the experiences we've had and the personality we were born with, is all somewhat intuitive. Let's switch things up a bit then. For the next half of the chapter, we will examine from the opposite side, as a parent and see if there is any new understanding we might have of faith through God's perspective.

Time for a confession. In the role of parent, I find it highly exasperating when my children don't trust me. When I reassure my son that there are no zombies under his bed, that I am entirely sure of this fact and ask him to believe me, and he instead gives into his irrational fears, I get frustrated. When my daughter misjudges her descent after climbing a tree and gets stuck on the lowest branch, and I tell her to jump, that I will catch her, and she instead panics and clings to the trunk in tears, I am annoyed. In those moments I've been known not to say the sweetest things as my patience evaporates. Please tell me you can think of a time that you were irritated when a child wouldn't trust your encouragement to do or try something you knew was possible?

I have to wonder why those experiences are so irritating? What do you think? If I look inwards, I find that I am not directing the irritation I feel at my children per se. It's usually the vexation of my selfish nature. With my son and his zombie fear, I know his lack of trust will crimp my evening plans, and with my daughter's stalling, it is the delay to my dinner prep that I dislike. In part then, some of my annoyance is pure selfish impatience that things aren't going as I planned.

There is something more there, though, then impatience. In my human emotions of frustration, I find a seed of empathy. When my daughter or son cry out in fear of something unreal or unlikely because they don't trust the truth I am sharing, I physically hurt because they are hurting. When they don't believe me, and they take onto themselves the burden that I am trying so hard to relieve, it is painful for me to watch, because I feel that burden with them.

Other times it is the empathy of regret because I know they are missing out on an opportunity that would be rewarding. When we go to the movies and buy a tub of buttery popcorn to share and my youngest's sighs at missing out on the snack, I feel an empathetic

24

squeeze, especially since I know he would probably enjoy it if he ever were brave enough to risk it.

How does all of this relate to God? For one, it's important to realize it isn't the same. That exasperating irritation I feel when non-trusting kids disrupt my plans is likely not something God feels. God isn't selfish in petty manners like me, so while my lack of trust on something may indeed delay His initial plan, He's not rolling His eyes at me for this. He just moves on to something or someone else if He needs.

I would guess, His frustration is more in line with the compassion and empathy I feel for my children when they don't trust. If I picture Him symbolically in the pool saying to me, "Jump, trust me, I've got you!" And I walk away. He must feel sad. He would know that I missed out not just on the experience itself, but a chance to increase my faith by learning He can be trusted. When my husband is out of town, and I start catastrophizing about him getting in a car accident, potentially dying, and leaving me alone to raise our kids, I'm sure God isn't upset that I don't readily turn to Him and trust His ultimate control. Instead, He feels compassion for the irrational fear that keeps me from sleeping. He wants to relieve my doubts if only I'd let Him.

Remember how much emphasis we placed on experiences having a lot to do with trust? This is such a crucial idea for increasing our faith. The Greek word used for faith or trust is *pistis*. Interestingly it comes from the Greek word *peitho* which means to persuade or be persuaded. When we are asking our kids to trust us on something, we are trying to convince them that it will be okay, that that they will have success, and that we know what we are talking about. One way that persuasion works is if they try it and find it to be true. The positive experience makes it easier to persuade them the next time.

This positive feedback loop is why God so longs for us to take the risk and find His words to be true, it makes the persuasion easier and makes our faith stronger. If you talk to anyone who has taken a leap of faith, and either chosen or been forced to trust God on something, they will tell you it makes the next time easier to trust. Usually, if you encounter someone who displays mighty faith, and by that, I mean that immediate reliance and turning to God without fear, you will find someone who has a handful of stories of God's faithfulness in the past. Their ability to trust without hesitation has come from repeated experiences of God coming through for them.

I can recall a couple during my teen years with earth-shattering faith. At first, I thought it was naive, that they trusted Him too much. How ridiculous does that sound now, as if there is such thing as too much faith! As I got to know them, I began to hear the stories that led to their incredible trust. Story after story of a need, often financial, that would miraculously be answered supernaturally. A check would appear for the exact amount needed to fix their car, or someone would arrive at their door with an old lawn mower they didn't need on the same day the couple prayed for a working lawnmower.

Now, for as many times as I get irked at my children for not trusting me on something of which I am confident, there are plenty of times they do believe me, and I must say, that feeling as a parent is just delightful. After several seasons at the lake encouraging my daughter to try to wakeboard, this past summer she finally decided to try. She's a gymnast, has excellent balance and strength, and I knew it would be easy for her to pick up. "Trust me," my husband and I both said to her over and over, "you can do this, and you will love it!"

Despite my outward confidence that I directed to my daughter of the success, she would have, since I am not God and not ultimately sure of how things will play out, I was inwardly quite nervous as my husband steadied her in the water behind the boat. She yelled, "Hit it," and I thrust the boat into gear, yanking my head back as quickly as I could to see what would happen. She popped right up, and the smile that lit up her face said it all. As a parent I saw so many things in her expression that day; pride in herself, the thrill of a new experience, gratitude that we'd pushed her to try, and even relief that she could indeed trust us.

That empathy part works both ways. I felt those same emotions with my daughter that day, and what a joy it was. God must take such delight when we finally take the risk and trust Him on something He tells us to believe that He will do.

There is one last concept that needs touching on in regard to trust. While it's true that experience and personality affect how quickly my children trust me, those things don't change my character or my responsibility to them as their parent, the object in whom they are putting their trust. Follow me on this, whether or not my kids follow through and trust my words, doesn't change the fact that I am trustworthy. My ability to catch them when they leap from the side of the pool has nothing to do with their faith in me. I will catch them, period, whether they believe I will or not.

In other words, our experiences and personality may influence how easy or hard it is to trust God, but God himself is unchanging and constant. Another way to say this is that my belief that a particular chair will hold me up or not, has nothing to do with the chair's actual ability to hold me. My trust or inability to trust the chair may change my actions, if I risk sitting or not, but the chair itself is constant.

God is trustworthy, true, good, all-powerful, merciful, etc. Whether I believe that or not, doesn't change God, it just changes my actions and reactions towards him.

The next time you find yourself hesitant to trust God on something, think of the parent/child relationship. In fact, right now, maybe you can think of something you know God has asked you to do or trust him on, that you are wavering on. Now think of a time you were trying to convince someone of something you were confident of. Gather up that inner feeling of assuredness and realize God feels that about what He's asking of you. I sometimes think if my children could just somehow feel the utter and most complete confidence I have when I say they can trust me to catch them, or that there are no such things as monsters, they wouldn't have doubt. If they only knew what I knew, they would trust easily.

God only asks for trust on things that are certain, and let's not fail to mention, He knows all. How much more must He think if they only could feel how concrete and sure this is, if only they knew what I know, they wouldn't need to doubt.

We will never be able to understand the assurance God possesses when He asks us to trust Him so that we will continue with our childlike faith. Childlike faith, an imperfect blend of moments of hesitancy, naivety, confidence, and courage. Hopefully, though, we will take more leaps of faith and continue to learn how faithful He is.

Chapter 3 **Discipline**

Most of us don't like the word discipline. It's not a warm fuzzy term, and for me has been one of the more challenging parts of parenting. There are several reasons it's been tough. For one, it doesn't seem as natural as nurturing. When one of my kids is hurt, some strange inner instinct takes over, and I find I don't have to think it through, I just comfort them. For discipline, it takes work and consistency to be effective. My instincts aren't always right, and I spend more time evaluating my actions then the actual discipline took to deliver. It is also something that is not appreciated at the moment. The reaction is never smiling and gratitude, but almost always resistance.

The other struggle with discipline is the distinctive styles we all bring to the table. What discipline style would you say you have? I wonder if it is different than other adults in your household. I don't seem to mind if my husband nurtures our kids in different ways than me, but for some reason when our styles clash on discipline techniques, sparks can fly!

Despite how much I may cringe at the idea of discipline, I have learned as a parent that it is necessary. We enter this world as selfish beings, and it's our natural state. We'll talk about this in a later chapter, but It Is precisely this act of being bent towards serving self that must be molded and managed.

I've already used the word discipline seven times, and yet it may be a good idea to define what the word means before we delve in deeper. The first part of the word discipline means to train, teach, or direct. That is palatable, and I don't think we have many problems with that concept. It's the part two that we don't like; using punishment to achieve the training. Punishment is defined as suffering, pain, or loss that serves as retribution, or it is defined as the penalty inflicted on the person who did the offense.

Discipline then is using a penalty, pain, suffering, or loss in attempts to train, teach, or direct someone. Can you think of why discipline is different than punishment? Punishment is the consequence without the desire to teach or help someone mature and be healthy. It's the hurt or pain without a plan forward. What's worse is when punishment degrades into cruelty or violence and becomes abuse. Please understand that we are talking about discipline and not abuse. It is a devastating fact that many of you have only experienced unhealthy discipline; power wielded to intimidate and belittle.

It is crucial also to mention here that behind the idea of good discipline, we expect a healthy relationship. In other words, I love my kids like crazy. I cannot separate that truth from our relationship. Thus, any correction or behavior changes I'm working on is assumed to come out of that love. My children must trust that fact implicitly; otherwise, discipline will be skewed into something harmful. Correction is not about power or perfect behavior. This is discipline that stems from wanting that absolute best for my kids.

From our working definition of discipline, let's encompass the words in the definition of punishment (penalty, loss, pain, etc.) into the word consequence. It's a term I hear more frequently than punishment and is easier to conceptualize with kids, either in a family, a school, church or other organization. Thus, discipline is training, teaching, and directing with the use of consequences.

Historically there are two types of consequences we talk about in discipline. One is external consequences, and the other is natural consequences. Remember at the start I mentioned that we all have different styles of discipline? Here is one place this comes to play. I would guess for you, doling out one of these types of consequences comes more naturally than the other. I know for me it does!

In our home, we try to use a mixture of the two types of consequences. An external consequence would be taking a privilege away, or the child is confined to their room. For example, my kids love dessert. Occasionally they get busy after dinner and forget that we have sweet morsels on our shelves, but this is very rare. Usually, it's the first request out of their mouths after they eat. The rule in our home is, you don't get dessert unless you finish the food on your plate. Invariably someone decides they don't like green beans or are so full they can't eat another bite. Yet the request is still there, "Can I have dessert?"

The behavior we want our kids to learn with this rule is being respectful of the meal provided, as well as learning healthy nutritional habits. The punishment of not getting dessert is the external measure or consequence we've implemented. This may not seem especially painful to you, trust me when I say that the tears spilled over this one rule have been very abundant over the years.

When I send one of my kids to their rooms, I am taking away the privilege of spending time with the rest of the family. We go on with our activities without the offending member, which, especially when they were young, was hard to endure. As they age, this time-out form of external consequence morphs into the age-old discipline of grounding.

Other ways discipline occurs is through natural consequences. This form of punishment seems more straightforward to dole out, and yet there is still a challenge. The challenge is not to intervene and rescue my child but allow the learning to occur through the painful outcome.

For instance, one of the traits we are training into our kids is responsibility. My daughter in the 4th grade is old enough to remember she has homework and to take the initiative to do that work. I will often prompt them when they get home from school, saying, "Does anyone have homework they need to do?" That is the extent, though, of my intervention. When we are walking out the door the next morning to school, and I hear a panicked, "I have homework!" It is time to for me to allow the natural consequences to occur. Yes, it is painful, and for my perfectionistic daughter, there will be tears, but training is happening before my eyes.

Additional examples of natural consequences have been eating an unfavorable school lunch because a child wanted to put off lunch making until we headed to the car for school, and "freezing" at recess because they refused to bring a jacket.

As a parent, I can tell you, that despite how challenging it is for me to be consistent and wise in my discipline decisions, the benefits are apparent. Over time, my children are gradually shaped into the type of beings that embody the character traits I and my husband value.

Again, it's not about behaving well. We are aiming for kind, respectful, compassionate, self-controlled people that will contribute in their unique way to the world. The external and natural consequences are the means of training and refining their dispositions.

Quite purposefully I haven't mentioned anything in regard to words and discipline. Had you noticed that? It's because whether it be lecturing, yelling, or threatening, words have insignificant effect in permanently changing behavior. When verbal power struggles entwine themselves with discipline, it usually has more to do with me feeling out of control. Thankfully, God doesn't lose control, so don't expect any long lectures or verbal threats from Him in your life.

I think we've dwelt enough on discipline with children and hopefully laid a useful framework for looking at God and discipline.

Now, why do you think, in general, people are uncomfortable with the theological concept that links God with discipline? I wonder if part of it is because, at first blush, they are removing the idea of a relationship with God, and assuming an authoritative, cold, uncaring figure is doling out punishment on a whim. I wouldn't like that kind of God either.

First then, like a parent, we must understand that any training in our lives that comes from God starts with the basis of love and relationship. The Bible mentions this idea in both the Old Testament and New Testament with the same words.

Proverbs 3:12 (NIV), "because the Lord disciplines those he loves, as a father the son he delights in."

Hebrews 12:6 (NIV), "because the Lord disciplines the one he loves, and chastens everyone he accepts as his son."

There is an excellent reason then we are looking at parents and kids to understand God and discipline; the Bible tells us it is precisely the same!

Second, like with our children, we must grasp that God isn't seeking perfect behavior, but is aiming for good character. The book of Hebrews goes on to mention this and verse 11 of chapter 12 states, "No discipline seems pleasant at the time, but painful. Later, however, it produces a harvest of righteousness and peace for those who have been trained by it." (NIV)

In that vein, I think we can see God's discipline as both external and natural consequences at play in our lives, being used to refine our nature. Hebrews mentions righteousness and peace as aims of his discipline, but as to individual character traits, what do you think God is perfecting us into? I could start a lengthy list here, but I wonder, could it be as simple as to be like Christ. Christ's nature or character is the nature he seeks for us. One way then to evaluate if the painful circumstances happening in your life are discipline, versus the pain we talked about in chapter one that comes from living on earth with other people, is to look for direct evidence it is pushing you towards more Christlikeness.

One of the many things He is working out inside me to become more Christlike is my ego. I am a prideful person and gravitate towards things that inflate my ego. A while back, I was serving as a chaplain for a woman's organization to which I belong to. As the months went by, I began to let any praise of the devotional I gave, feed my pride. We had a joint meeting with another group scheduled, and I remember thinking inwardly how much I was going to enjoy wowing the other group with my devotion. Leave it to God to know I needed some discipline. I came to that joint meeting ready to impress, only to find that the chaplain from the other group was giving the devotional. I honestly believe that evening I experienced an external consequence for my pride. Just as I take away the privilege of dessert sometimes for my kids, God took away the opportunity of speaking that night. It was painful to go through the process of having that pride illuminated, and it's icky! But I needed that external consequence to wake me up!

God also works through natural consequences to discipline us. Like with my daughter and her homework, this is less about physical punishment and more God not intervening and not rescuing. At times this may be genuine discomfort or even illness from poor decisions I've made. A natural consequence of speaking unkindly about someone may be the loss of a relationship or having unkind things said about me, either of which would be painful.

I may want God to rescue me from an overburdened schedule, but he likely will allow me to feel the stress and frenzy of it all, to hopefully discipline me in the art of saying no. I may want God to rid my mind of a scary image from a horror movie I shouldn't have watched, but he likely will allow me to experience the consequential fear for a few weeks, to guide me away from further harm.

There is something else we can learn about parenthood, discipline, and God. While I have allowed painful and external consequences for my kids, I have never as a parent arbitrarily caused pain. This is extremely important to differentiate.

One example of this would be when my two-year-old went through the process of learning that fire is dangerous and can hurt. I had watched him express interest in candles and flames in our fireplace for weeks. I felt I was always hovering, pulling him out of harm's way and scolding him verbally. One day he was examining a burning candle, and I had gone through the "No, hot!" lingo several times while moving his finger away. He wasn't getting It. I decided to let him burn himself. I decided to allow a natural consequence of touching fire to occur. His little finger went towards the flame, and I repeated my admonishing but didn't intervene. The reaction was immediate, he burst out into tears at the pain of the heat, and I swept him up and kissed his finger and told him how sorry I was. I don't even think the flame honestly burned him, but I can tell you I never had to correct him or scold him again when it came to fires. He learned, and the heat trained him well.

While I allowed that hurt in a monitored situation, I would never randomly burn my children to teach them about a fire. Such unpredictable harm would serve no purpose in the realm of training or teaching. It's the same with God, hear me on this, he does not capriciously hurt us with the hope we may "learn" something. God does not dole out tragedy as a discipline.

I may allow my kids to crash into each other when they are running too fast in the house and let the natural consequence of their speed to teach them to slow down, but I would not externally shove them into each other as a form of training or discipline. A natural consequence of smoking 40 years may be lung cancer, but trust me, God does not give cancer to people to punish or discipline them. God does not arbitrarily strike cities with natural disasters or plunge airplanes into the ground to teach us, humans, a lesson.

As a parent, I realize how necessary discipline is. Without any correction, my kids' natural tendency would be self-serving. If there was never any external consequences and I rescued them from any natural consequences, I would, in turn, be raising selfish, entitled, uncaring, uncompromising, dependent beings who in all likelihood wouldn't be able to transition into adulthood. Not only that, my guess is they wouldn't be very happy or fulfilled. I love my children, and can only hope they will find meaning, contentment, and joy in life. To increase those odds, I must do the challenging work of training now.

How do I know this? Because I am a flawed human being who at times has tried the easy way out and instead of discipline, I've rescued or let a boundary go. I've been the parent who's allowed overindulgence in screen time. No limitations with a time limit may have initially brought delight to my little ones, but I can tell you at the end of those days, my kids are miserable.

God too, wants the best for us. He wants us to have joy, peace, and purpose. Like a parent, he loves us enough to go through the hard work of discipline, despite the temporary pain it may cause.

One last little metaphor I wanted to mention. If you are a parent, you know that no two children are the same. It was a shock to me to realize that the discipline technique that had worked so well for my daughter did not work at all for my son. My introvert son would find it a reward to be banished to his room, while the extroverted son finds this to be the worst punishment in the world. Part of being a parent and learning the unique make-up of my kids is tailoring the training to them individually.

God does the same with us. There is an obscure scripture that talks about this. Isaiah 28:24-29 talks about a farmer and his crops.

The verses point out that this farmer treats the crops differently, both in sowing and in harvesting. Caraway is beaten with a rod, cumin a stick and grain must be ground. The description ends with, "All this also comes from the Lord Almighty, whose plan is wonderful, whose wisdom is magnificent." (verse 29) We are all so different, and God who is wise and wonderful knows me so well, that correction for my character is tailor designed.

One final thought, which is highly relevant to touch on. If you've been around kids and have needed to correct a behavior, you probably understand that the child also has a role in that discipline. They have a choice (free will) on how they respond to consequences. If I give my daughter a warning look, and she decides in that instant to course correct, then nothing else needs to be done. This, of course, would be ideal, and I wish all my kids could just learn from looks. However, if she ignores the visual warning, and ignores the verbal caution, and even resists the external consequence, the discipline is going to escalate. Our supplication versus our refusal to change may also play a part in God's discipline. I don't know about you, but I'd rather have the visual warning from God over the potential escalation of my ignoring His gentle correction.

It is this fact that may cause some of the discrepancies you notice with discipline and God. We often think how harsh God was dealing with the Israelites in the Old Testament, but perhaps that was the escalation of ignored mild consequences. Maybe you've seen more severe discipline in your life or someone you love, and you think it's not fair. Could it just be that they disregarded the other attempts?

Though we may be uncomfortable with the idea of a disciplining God, I think our experience of discipline within a family structure can help us conceptualize it, and ultimately even be grateful for it. We must always know it's meant to form and guide us into something more significant and given by a God who is good and wise. In fact, it's more evidence of how much He genuinely adores us.

Chapter 4 **Free Will**

There are many times that I wish I could make all the decisions for my children. It would be so much easier if I could just choose what they wear to school, how they fix their hair, what they eat for the day, which friends they want to spend time with. Don't get me wrong, I have input on these things, but ultimately, I leave the choice up to them.

There are some reading this who are balking at the idea of letting your child pick out their clothes or food for breakfast. I know every family is different in how much or little control they allow their children to have, but the fact is our children still have their little wills that exert control over situations. Even if you make decisions about dress, meals, appearance, I would guess there are times that there has been pushback from a child with a different opinion.

Deep down, don't we sense that our role as parents is more than just protecting our children from the wrong choices, that in actuality we are trying to help them develop into good decision makers? It is easy for me to get caught up in the moment and focus on controlling their choices to protect them immediately. Somewhere inside of me, though, there is a naggling that ultimately, I want them to be in control of their lives and make right choices. The only way to learn what good choices are is through lots and lots of practice making wrong decisions when the consequences are easily managed.

This idea of free will, or the ability to have control over decisions, is central to the Christian faith. Without choice, there would be no relationship with our creator. We would just be workers or servants doing the bidding of our God. And yet, it is that ability to choose that opens up so many conundrums within theology and faith.

As mentioned in the first chapter, it is this ability to decide things for ourselves that causes much of the pain and suffering we encounter in life. One of the things I've had to wrestle with in the realm of free will is what role God plays in knowing and yet not controlling our decisions. One of the many attributes God possesses is that he is omniscient, or all-knowing. The question then becomes, if he already knows what we will decide is it genuinely free choice?

I think parenting provides an inkling into what this might look like for God.

For breakfast each morning I ask my kids what they want. Some of you shudder at this freedom, how crazy must I be to let my kids decide! Those of you who just serve what you think is best and most healthy, probably envision chaos with free choice. In fact, I think people who prefer control over these types of little decisions are trying to avoid what they believe would happen if their kids decided things; mayhem, disorder, complication!

I can understand the fear. I have three kids, so the potential of different options for breakfast could be enormous, and it could take much of my morning catering to each child's preference. But here's the funny thing that's happened in time. They've become predictable and routine. They have probably ten choices; frozen waffle, frozen pancake, breakfast corndog (yes there is such a thing), toaster strudel, toast, several types of cereal, oatmeal, eggs, yogurt, etc. Without fail, though, each child chooses the same thing every day.

It makes me chuckle when I ask, "What do you want for breakfast?", and they reply, "the usual." You must realize that just because I know almost certainly what they will choose doesn't mean they don't have free choice; it merely means I know them well.

It's not just breakfast food choices that are predictable. I can also predict what they will choose to wear to school, which child will protest on wearing a coat and which child will need prodding to keep on task. Depending on what time they woke up, or their first few words to me in the morning, I can guess if there will be tears or fights or frantic scurrying before school versus those beautifully rare mornings when they seem to like each other, and calm envelops us as we step out of the house.

You do this too, don't you? You begin to be able to predict choices and actions of people you are around frequently. Usually, the more we know someone, the more we can anticipate what action, behavior, or even words they may respond with. If I can foresee accurately hundreds of things my kids say and do, though they've just been with me years at this point, how much greater can God, who is my creator, know and predict what choices I am going to make.

The first point then is that just because someone can predict a decision you are going to make, doesn't mean you don't have free will. Not only that, but the more you know someone, the more confident you can be that you truly know what choice they will make. God's omniscience, which is perfect and total, doesn't change the fact that we still have free will.

Now, there are a couple of considerations to make about this vast "knowing" that relates to me as a parent and then ultimately transcends to our understanding of God. One, because of the knowledge I have of my children, some of the advice and boundaries I dole out are unique to my children as individuals. For instance, one of my kids is super sensitive to caffeine. If we are splurging on pop for a meal out, this child cannot have a drink with caffeine. It's a unique boundary for him.

I think there are times God may give a specific boundary for us, knowing that the potential for harm is unique for us as individuals.

Other times, in knowing a particular struggle or weak spot for one of my kids, I'll set a standard for all of them to follow. One of my boys has a tough time getting scary images out of his mind from movies. I've had him come to me, fearful because something he watched a year ago is haunting his mind. It's easier, now that I know this about him, to limit scary content for all three of them. It's true the others aren't affected in the same way, but it's not worth causing him harm by either being excluded from family movies or adding more nightmare material to his repertoire.

There are stipulations like this in the Bible as well, general things God has said to watch out for, because it may cause a brother or sister to falter.

This is the first consideration; the more I know and understand my children, the better tailored my encouragement and guidelines are for them. They still have their own choices and decisions to make, and I can predict the impact of those choices. However, because I love them and don't enjoy watching them suffer, I try to offer guidance to provide and protect them on their journey of choice making. This advice or boundary setting is at times unique to them as individuals, and at other times the standards for all three are set to shield just one.

Here is the second consideration; despite being able to predict most of their decisions, both good and bad, I am always hoping and rooting for them to make the best choice. Part of that relationship of love means that I want goodness for them, and I believe in their best potential selves. Thus, even when they are sleep deprived and on a sugar high, running around the home like banshees, I know they have the potential to make a good choice when I say, "Okay, time to go brush your teeth and get ready for bed."

I know they are capable of saying, "Sure thing!" and walking calmly to the bathroom, taking turns with the sink, cleaning up any overzealous toothpaste squirts, changing into PJs and putting dirty clothes away and climbing into bed. It's what I hope for every night. There must be a part of me that expects that because I'm surprised when it doesn't happen. Surprised, and yet, not surprised. It's as if I hold both realities in me at the same time. One is the potential, and one is probable.

I would guess God does this on an infinitely vaster plane. He holds both the potential and the probable for our decisions within him at every moment. He is forever optimistic that we will follow the right path. This truth is written all over the old testament, from the very beginning.

When I say beginning, I really mean the beginning. Let's look at the very first example of free will gone awry in the Bible. Genesis 2:16-17 (NIV) says, "And the Lord God commanded the man, "You are free to eat from any tree in the garden; but you must not eat from the tree of the knowledge of good and evil, for when you eat from it you will certainly die."

The setup is much like what we experience with our children. There is a boundary in place, with complete freedom to make decisions inside or outside of that limit. Adam and Eve use their free will to choose disobedience, eating from the tree that will eventually cause death. Do you think God was surprised by their choice? If He holds both the probable and potential, then I suppose we could say He was surprised and not surprised.

More examples of God's optimism in the midst of his omniscience comes in Judges chapter 2. We read that over a period of 350 years, the nation of Israel went through a cycle of rejecting God, being enslaved as a consequence, repenting, and being restored. This cycle occurred at least 12 times in Judges. Again, and again. Over and Over. And yet, don't you think God was like we are as parents, each time genuinely hoping they would make right decisions, yet fully aware of the likelihood of disaster.

42

This idea of perfect knowing coupled with the hope of potential change can be tough to wrap our minds around when it comes to God and free will, especially if we think of it as concrete and fixed. Here again, we can turn to parent and children interactions to see the fluidity of omniscience.

The ability as a parent for me to predict my children's behavior is continually shifting. It's not static by any means, but changes with each action they choose. When they pick which friend is coming over to play, I begin to visualize how the time may go and how involved I'll need to be. One particular friend and my son have a more contentious relationship, so if this friend comes over, I can already predict I will be intervening to keep the peace and may have more consoling to do after. It's not just who he invites that changes things. As whichever friend arrives, I will evaluate both their moods as well as see what activity they decide to do. Their attitudes and choices continue to change my expectations. Going outside to shoot baskets doesn't require as much from me as deciding to do a science experiment in the kitchen does. I'm in a constant state of predicting, so I can plan for potential and probable problems.

God is constantly shifting his predictions of our choices too, but with one added benefit. This benefit allows him to do this perfectly; He is omniscient. God is in the past, present, and future simultaneously. And yet, though He is unchanging, it is precisely our free will that makes this something very dynamic for Him. In a much grander sense then, He holds both what is and what He hopes will be in every moment.

My little brain can't mentally grasp God's abilities, so the parenting example of holding both what I expect and what I wish for my kids in their day to day choices is the best I can do for understanding the concept of omniscience as it relates to faith. In other words, a faith that requires free will to ensure autonomy and ultimately a choice to have a relationship with our creator is not nullified by that creator's ability to know everything. In fact, his omniscience, coupled with how intimately he knows me, allows for complete guidance and direction individually.

Chapter 5 **Hope & Disappointment**

Hope is one of those words we use all the time. "I hope you have a great day!" is something I said just this morning as I dropped my kids off at school. Think of all the things we say we hope for; I hope it snows, I hope you aren't late again, I hope you feel better soon, etc. The response, "I hope so," is a well-worn track that is spewed out to both the most trivial and the most complex statements. The hope that my son doesn't come home with another hole in the knee of his pants is altogether different than hoping my friend's lump she found isn't cancer. The words are the same, but the desire behind those situations is much different.

Now think of the word wish. Do you think of wish and hope as the same thing? To help you work through the differences, think of something you wish for and something you hope for. How likely to come to pass are each of those things? There should be a difference, as there is an expectation in the outcome with a hope that wishing just doesn't have.

I may wish that I would win the lottery, but I don't expect to, which makes it more of a wish than hope. We use the words so interchangeably, however, that it adds to the confusion of the theological concept of hope. Merriam-Webster distinguishes a wish from hope by stating that wishing is, "to have a desire for something unattainable," which contrasts with hope as "to expect with confidence." See the difference? One is a dream, and one is an expectation.

In the realm of parenting hope is the promise of potential change. We discussed in the chapter about free will that the thing that keeps me sane is holding both the probable and potential in mind with my kids as they make choices in their day. Hope is the half of me that expects the right behavior, and it is grace that accepts the wrong behavior.

Hope we might say comes before the outcome, and grace is a response to the outcome.

As humans, many would say that hope is necessary. We spend so much energy creating, protecting, and looking for hope that we forget it is a crucial aspect of God's nature as well. To fully grasp how God embraces hope for us let us examine our children.

Off the cuff, what are some specific hopes you have for either your children or other children in your life? Recall that hope is confidently expecting something. For me, I hope that my kids have a vibrant relationship with Christ. I hope that they find peace and joy in their lives. I hope that they reach their potential of who God created them to be. I hope they will be not only redeemed but restored from whatever harms they may encounter.

I admit, at times my hopes for them waver into secular values such as hope for love, financial stability, respect, and happiness, I am aware that those can be fleeting and ultimately unfulfilling without a relationship with Christ first and foremost.

Notice in both lists that I didn't mention anything about hoping they are the most attractive, most athletic, most intelligent, or most successful people. Behind those hopes is the desire for them to have value based on external measures, which in turn would bring value to me as their parent. What's wrong with these types of hopes, you ask?

The risk of using our children as objects to put our hope in to give our lives meaning and purpose.

Perhaps you have seen examples of this, where a parent has placed their hope in the success of their child in sports, or academics, or popularity, or career. Hope *in* our children is not the same as hope *for* our children.

Hope in and of itself is extremely persistent. When I think about the hopes I have for my children, I know I will never give up on those promises. In fact, as a thought experiment, I have pushed myself to see if there is a limit to this hope I have for them. Would I give up on them finding peace and restoration, even if they committed a heinous crime? No. If they disowned me as their mother, and walked out of my life for good, vowing to never speak to me again, would I abandon my hope for reconciliation? No.

Why is that? Because I love them unconditionally, and they are mine. Here's the thing, God loves us unconditionally, and we are His. God maintains hope for our salvation and reconciliation no matter what we've done or how far away we've gone. This, of course, is what we have been leading up to; If I don't ever give up on my children, God absolutely will never give up on us.

Chapter 15 in the book of Luke records three stories Christ tells about lost things. There is a lost sheep, a lost coin, and a lost son. In each story, the seeker perseveres until he finds the sheep and coin, and the son comes home. What is it that keeps the seeker, seeking? Hope. It is hope that accompanies the one who is searching and makes perseverance possible. Christ tells the parables to illustrate not just His grace and mercy but His determination. Behind His unending pursuit is His eternal hope, which allows Him to never give up on us.

Think in your own life how important hope is to perseverance. As a parent, it was the hope that my children would someday sleep through the night that helped me plod through some rough sleep deprived periods of parenting. It is the hope that my children will one day broaden their palates that keeps me fixing and trying new foods. It is the hope that they will one day learn to be kind to each other that helps me not pull out all my hair in daily bouts of parenting failures.

It's time to add in some reality. Up to this point, we've been in "*pre*" mode, talking about things in the future that we expect or are confident will occur. As human beings that have lived for at least a few years or decades, we know that it's not unusual for something we hope for to not work out. Despite the confidence we may have had, things don't always go how we planned.

So, what happens when circumstances or people do not meet our expectations? When our hopes don't come to fruition? Or worse when we have epic failures or a devastating loss? Depending on what the expectations were, we may be crushed and traumatized, but undoubtedly at the least, we will experience disappointment. Disappointment is what is at the heart of unfulfilled hopes and is a potent emotion. In fact, even the mere threat of disappointment will often influence our actions.

How often have you heard people say that the reason behind their behavior is to avoid disappointing someone? A lot of the choices I made in my teen years to not break my parent's rules, was less about agreeing with their parameters, and more about trying not to disappoint them. It's more than just childhood behavior that is affected by fear of letting others down, our aversion to disappointing others is responsible for many current commitments and time-consuming activities, emotions, and thoughts.

The reason for this is that we tie disappointment to disapproval. I know that some of my decisions to be involved in specific projects or take on different roles is due to the fear of disappointing and ultimately losing the approval of someone. Can you pinpoint things you've done or not done, based on trying to prevent disappointment and disapproval?

This creates a problem spiritually. We deal with disappointment so often in our families and with our relationships that we try to carry this same threat over to our relationship with God. In other words, because I experience the feeling of disappointment when I catch my son playing a violent video game after we talked about the potential harm, I assume God must be disappointed in me when I fill my brain with movie filth when I know the possible damage. Or because I feel intense disappointment in myself when I do something I promised myself I wouldn't do, I naturally expect God must be feeling that same disappointment in me.

Have you ever felt that God was disappointed in you? That because as humans our response to failure is often disappointment, that God's response to our failures must be the same?

What if I told you it's not the same! Did you know that never once in the Bible does God use the word disappointment concerning His people? He never states He is disappointed in us. In fact, I would argue it is impossible for Him to be disappointed in us.

That's right, impossible. To conceptualize this, we have to bring hope back into the picture. If we were to write out an equation for this, it would look like this: hope (expectation) + unmet expectation = disappointment.   Remember hope is having confidence and expecting something to occur, and when it doesn't, we are hurt and sad.

I'm going to add the other human element to this equation that explains its truth: hope (expectation) + unmet expectation (surprise) = disappointment. You see, disappointment holds hands with surprise because in life the future is unknown. It is the unexpected unfulfilled expectation that hurts.

When one of my children says something disrespectful, it is the surprise coupled with the letdown that causes the disappointment. When I hope I will get the job after a stellar interview, my disappointment at being passed over is related to the outcome being unanticipated. Obviously, if I had known at the outset I wouldn't get the job, I wouldn't have had hope or expectations for the job, and thus wouldn't have been disappointed.

So, disappointment occurs when our hopes are dashed by something unforeseen. Unlike humans, though, nothing is a surprise to God. Herein lies the grand difference between God and man, because everything is already known, God can't have expectations that aren't met, and therefore He can't be disappointed.

One of my friends told me about a moment her son disappointed her, years ago. She had hoped he would get through his High School years without any underage drinking. She was confident in his sound choices until she was surprised one morning to find him hung over from a party. She retold how discouraged she was and displeased with him because she knew his potential.

I asked her, "Looking back now at that day and knowing what you know about him today, would you still be as disappointed?"

She didn't even hesitate, "Well no, because now I know it didn't make a difference. Even if it had, if there had been some consequence, I know now the kind of person he is, and I wouldn't have reacted the same."

I clarified further, "So, if all those years ago, if I could have told you before the event that, one your son was going to slip up one night and drink, and two he is going to grow in character from the poor choice he made, would you have experienced disappointment?"

She smiled, "No, I suppose not. If I knew the future, then it wouldn't have bothered me, and maybe I would have been glad it happened as it did."

Let's say we watch a movie for the first time and find ourselves disappointed in the decisions the characters make along the way. But then we reach the end, and it all works out, and more importantly the characters grow and learn from their choices and are better people for them. My guess is, if we watch that movie a second time, knowing the outcome and without surprises, we wouldn't feel disappointed in those same decisions.

God can live in all time and already knows every microsecond how we will respond, both good and bad, and how He can use those moments to refine us that allows for the inability to be disappointed. He is never surprised (He's already seen the movie and knows how it ends)!

Romans 8:28 says, "And we know in all things God works for the good of those who love him, who have been called according to his purpose." (NIV). Not only is he not disappointed because he's not surprised, but he's also actually working with each decision and experience in our lives for something good. It's important to note that the Greek word used here for good is *agathos* which means good as in essential goodness, or good in nature, kind, generous. Think opposite of evil. In other words, God is trying for a good character (internal) and not good circumstances (external).

This constant working for good, is how he can view our lives with such profound hope. His confidence in us and in our ability to be redeemed is why he never stops pursuing and giving opportunities for healing and growth. I don't know about you, but that reassurance is something I need often.

As a parent who experiences both hope and disappointment with my kids, conceptualizing how God encompasses only the hope side, has helped me to not overreact to life's failures. It's a process, but I have to remind myself that I don't know the ending. Trying to wrap my brain around the idea that God already knows the ways I'm going to mess up and fail and is not disappointed, but instead already working to use those defeats to refine me fills me with hope!

If God is doing this with me, He's also doing it with my children. If I can just hold onto that reality, perhaps I can parent with more hope and less disappointment, more grace and less condemnation.

Chapter 6 **Judgment**

If we are really honest, there are several words in the Bible we just don't like to dwell on. One of those words or ideas is Judgement. This is especially true of people who are not a part of the Christian faith. How many times have you heard someone say that they think Christians are too judgmental? It's a common complaint about Christianity, and in fact, many use it as one of the reasons they don't want to attend church or embrace Christianity.

I'll tell you what perplexes me. The secular world claims we do this too much, and yet, Christians aren't supposed to be judgmental at all! Countless scriptures warn us not to judge. Do you want an example? Matthew 7:1 (NIV) is about as straightforward as you can get, saying, "Do not judge, or you too will be judged." If we are told not to judge others, how have Christians gained a reputation for being judgmental? Often Christians argue that it's something that can't be helped, that by knowing right and wrong, we naturally judge, and it is our right to do so.

It's time to look to children to get a better understanding of why judgment is something Christ tells us not to do.

If you've been around kids for anytime, you know that they judge often and naturally. Kids do this because it is necessary for learning. We are designed to interact with our world through categories. Thus, as developing infants, their little minds start separating things very early. When my daughter was seven months old, she could tell the difference between a dog (something alive) and a car (something we travel in), but she would not have been able to separate out a German Shepherd from a Golden Retriever.

When my daughter first began to speak, Wa-wa was any liquid that she could drink. In her brain, she had already separated out liquids from solids. In time she would differentiate water, milk, and juice. You see though that categorizing is a necessary part of human thinking.

The process of noticing differences is what we call distinguishing or differentiating. This ability is absolutely a component of being human. It is also something that develops as we age. I'm sure many of us have gone through the heartwarming stage when our children literally could not distinguish skin tone differences. The problem with the sweet idea that we should somehow preserve the ability not to notice if someone has dark skin or light skin is that it is impossible. Between the ages 3 and 5, although not understanding the concept of race or ethnicity, kids become aware of skin tone differences.

One can hone the skill of awareness of differences as well. Think of people we say have a distinguished palette. With that label, we acknowledge that certain individuals can differentiate tastes and textures the rest of us aren't even aware of.

Differentiating and noticing differences in the world around us to categorize things, is not the same as judgment. Making a distinction between them is crucial. (Look, I'm using the skill of differentiation in real time). These two concepts differ in that judgment adds a layer to the separation by adding the element of morality. Judgement looks at something and decides if it is good or bad. It takes distinguishing to another level by finding fault in the difference.

Pronouncing failures, unfortunately, is where my children seem naturally gifted. They quickly find fault with each other and in people outside of our home. It was alarming the first time my daughter loudly pointed out a man with long hair as we shopped for groceries. "Mom!" she said dramatically, "That man has hair like a girl. What's wrong with him?" My embarrassment was evident in the immediate red hue to my face and quick about-face with our cart to a different aisle. The issue wasn't that she had merely noticed a man with long hair, which didn't fit in her category of male and female at that young age, it was that she had immediately found fault with this man, and in her mind, he was wrong.

As they age, children judge less on physical features and look more at behavior. As early as pre-school my kids would rattle off a story of someone getting in trouble from class, and I'd hear "He's the bad kid." Or else they'd alert me to how horrible it was that their friend was allowed to watch "R" rated movies or was overheard saying an inappropriate word. The problem with these stories is that my children were not merely discriminating or placing behavior in a category of what our family permitted or did not. They added judgment, and in their descriptions conveyed a moral critique. The theme of their stories was to let me know what a bad person these people were and therefore what a good person they were for not doing those things.

It's even worse in our home, where each of my children feels the need to point out each other's flawed behavior continually. "He didn't pick up his dirty clothes last night," "She doesn't have her seatbelt on," "He stuck out his tongue at me!" They point out these errors to me to suggest their sibling is in the wrong; therefore, they are in the right.

Now we get to the reason why it's so easy to judge; it protects our concept of self as worthy as we relate to others. By placing someone else in the wrong, it lifts us into the right. When we set judgment on someone else and make them "bad," it alternatively makes us "good."

It's easy in the role of a parent to see how ridiculous their judging is. I point this fact out daily to them; their friend is not evil for saying that word or watching that movie. Their sibling isn't morally corrupt for sneaking a second dessert, or not doing their homework. But it's not just that; it's that I don't love my children more or less based on this information. When the tattling starts, I protest, "I don't care!" Because I literally don't care! You would surely think that they understand at this point, that my love doesn't increase and decrease based on if they did their chores or not, or based on who started the fight.

Our quick judgments of others tells me that a part of us must believe God's affection changes based on what we do or don't do. Just like my kids trying to convince me of their worthiness by pointing out the fault of another, we try to convince God of our worthiness by finding errors in others. God views us all in the same way! Our behavior doesn't affect how much He loves us.

One reason Christians judge then, is that they haven't fully connected with the idea of God's unconditional love. If we do grasp that our worthiness in Christ is unrelated to our behaviors, why else might we find ourselves judging others? If I am "good" in God's eyes, then for me to look at someone else's life, and decide what they are doing is wrong and find fault in their actions, the only benefit it serves is to make me feel better about myself. In other words, the second reason is a self-confidence or self-assurance issue.

There is a third reason we may find ourselves judging others, and that is to avoid our faults. Unfortunately, when we focus on other's errors, it brings us a false sense of merit. I love the parable Jesus tells after commanding us not to judge in Matthew, as it illustrates this perfectly.

"Why do you look at the speck of sawdust in your brother's eye and pay no attention to the plank in your own eye? How can you say to your brother, 'Let me take the speck out of your eye,' when all the time there is a plank in your own eye?" Matthew 7: 3-4 (NIV)

He asks, how can we do this? We do this, so we don't have to pay attention to our own faults. "Look at that speck in his life! That is bad! Thank goodness that's not me! No sawdust in here!"

Avoiding our flaws is another reason why He tells us not to judge. We are to be concerned with our own lives. I say to my children the same thing; "Worry about yourself.", I must proclaim at least ten times a day.

Let's review. Judgement differentiates people, things, behavior, etc. into right/wrong, good/bad. As an individual, I judge others to try to make myself appear worthier before God, or to make me feel better about myself, or to ignore true wrongs in my life. Because all of these reasons are ultimately harmful to both ourselves and others, God commands us not to judge.

There is something else I have learned about the concept of judgment from my kids, and that is how easily we can make errors in our judgements. My son told me about a boy at school who stole another kid's chips from his lunchbox and was judged by his peers as a bad kid. Guess what? He was just hungry. His single mom had lost her job, and they hadn't had food in the house for days. Although my son was quick to judge and define this boy as evil, once the whole story was known, suddenly the stealing didn't seem as wrong. As the adult, I knew that background. If I had to play the role of judge in this scenario, my conclusion of guilt or not would be determined by knowing the whole story. I don't know about you, but if I need to be judged on something, I sure want someone who knows me well and knows the whole story to be the judge!

Don't think it's just kids who get it wrong! One of the dearest friendships I have almost didn't happen due to false judgment. My first interaction with her was at a ladies church crafting event. She had just moved to town and bragged to the other women that instead of unpacking she'd spent the week binging on sweets and a TV series called "Army Wives." She described her home vividly, depicting a chaotic unkempt disaster and neglected kids. My judgment was swift. Internally I decided she was a sloth, addicted to TV and food, not a good mother, and clearly without "righteous" values. We will never be friends, I thought, inflating my merit pridefully above her.

Oh, how wrong I was. I know now that the week she described had been a week of isolated depression after moving to a new community. She is so utterly the opposite of all my snap judgments that retelling this story always brings us to tears of laughter. So many of the judgments we make about others are wrong because we don't know the whole story.

The good news? God always knows the whole story. It is His perfect knowledge of all things and His totality of understanding our inner selves that allows Him to be the only one who should judge. James 4:12 (NIV) says this well, "There is only one Lawgiver and Judge, the one who is able to save and destroy. But you- who are you to judge your neighbor?"

God tells us not to judge others not only because it distracts us from the truth of ourselves and the reality of God's love and compassion, but because we are imperfect in our ability to entirely know and understand the choices others make.

Watching my children has taught me a lot about judgment. I realize how not seeing the whole picture frequently gets in the way of accurate assessments. I also see more clearly the reasons behind judging, and as I watch my kids dish out judgment on each other I see how they are trying to increase their own sense of being good.

We will always distinguish and differentiate things; it's how we think and learn. My children must be able to evaluate whether an action they take is harmful or beneficial, whether their behavior was selfish or not, etc. We must do this, too. What we are asked to avoid, however, is the blame and shame part. We shouldn't view ourselves or others as unworthy because of the actions we commit.

Chapter 7 **Prayer**

Did you ever notice how quickly a fun conversation with curious little 4 and 5-year-olds can take a dramatic turn into profound mind-stumping silence? "Who did Adam and Eve's kids marry if they were the only humans?" "Were people alive when the dinosaurs roamed?" "How come I've never heard God's voice speak to me when I pray?"

I try hard to satisfy their questions. Sometimes the answers are so abstract that their little minds can't grasp my feeble responses. Other times I don't know the answer and have to reply, "I have wondered that too!" Despite the initial panic when they ask about these deep curiosities, I love their questions and will always encourage them to think and ask whatever things come to their minds.

In my brief stent being a parent, the idea of prayer is a topic that has gotten a lot of questions. To be honest, it's a challenging concept for adults to conceptualize as well. I recall a night I was putting my three-year-old daughter to bed. As was typical I took her little hand in mine and told her it was time to pray. This particular night, I asked her if she wanted to pray first. I was shocked by her immediate, "NO!" Her face looked a bit frightened, and I asked her why she didn't want to talk to God? She scrunched her eyes and put her head down in embarrassment and explained she didn't know what to say to him. I gave her some examples of things she could say, like thank you, or I love you or help me to sleep with no nightmares. She continued to look squeamish and said emphatically, "Mom, I can't do that. It seems too weird to talk out loud like that.

Inwardly I felt like somehow, I must be failing as a parent if my children were too shy to pray or just plain refused to talk to God.

I've had many more discussions about prayer with all my kids, usually surrounding two main topics. First, they want to know what prayer is, and question why we speak to someone we cannot see or hear. And two, they struggle with requests, especially not understanding when something they ask for doesn't happen. I would guess these are two areas adults struggle with as well, so let's turn it around and look at it through our interactions with parents and kids.

At its most basic what is prayer? Prayer is essentially communication. Whether spoken inwardly or externally, with actual words or an aching soul, prayer is the way in which we commune with God. What do we know about communication? In our earthly lives, it is how we gain understanding. It is through dialogue we express needs, wants, feelings, and knowledge. While communication is the vehicle for these things, the result is comprehension, awareness, and ultimately "knowing."

As a parent, much of the intimate knowledge of my children have come through these verbal interactions. With their words, I have learned the things they dislike and the things they are passionate about. I hear their complaints, fears, and hopes. I get glimpses of what they think of themselves, both good and bad. These conversations build our relationship, all of it; the minutiae, the pleadings, the prideful boasts, and dramatic complaints. Whether it's arguing, honest questions, gratitude, or just telling me about their day, it ultimately brings us closer together.

It's the same with our prayers to God, which is just communication. Every bit of our interaction with God brings us closer. Oswald Chambers says of prayer in <u>My Utmost for His Highest</u>, "We look upon prayer simply as a means of getting things for ourselves, but the Biblical purpose of prayer is that we may get to know God Himself."

In theory, this idea that prayer is communication, and one part of a conversation is building a better understanding of each other, sounds simple to grasp. However, it is still hard to feel comfortable doing this with someone or something you cannot physically see. All I can say is that the more you speak to God as if he were present (which he is!), the easier it becomes.

Prayer then is a means to build a relationship and intimacy with God, but it is also clear Biblically that request is a part of prayer as well. There are countless verses in the New Testament that mention this concept.

Let's read some examples: Matthew 7:11 (NIV), "If you, then, though you are evil, know how to give good gifts to your children, how much more will your Father in heaven give good gifts to those who ask Him!"

Mark 11:24 (NIV), "Therefore I tell you, whatever you ask for in prayer, believe that you have received it, and it will be yours.

" Ephesians 6:18 (NIV), "And pray in the Spirit on all occasions with all kinds of prayers and requests. With this in mind, be alert and always keep on praying for all the Lord's people."

The take away from these verses is that we should request and ask for things. When I think about the idea of petitioning God, it's helpful for me to consider my role as a parent with kids who ask for things regularly. My children are free to ask and request anything. They have learned, however, that asking and receiving are two different matters.

When it comes to actual gifts, like the verses in Matthew, I do love giving them good things. I lowever, it is with the wisdom of maturity as their parent, that I decide what gift to give.

My youngest once very seriously asked for a cement truck. Not a toy, an actual cement truck. The reason was sweet; he wanted the cement to lay down a train track so that he could have the ability to visit his friend by train, who lived across town. A more appropriate gift, in this case, was to arrange a playdate.

We do the same with God. In my son's eyes, the cement truck was a sincere and earnest request, one he was sure would solve his problem. We often think we know exactly what God should give us to answer a longing in our heart. His wisdom, though, is far greater than our desires, and trust me, he will find a way to meet that longing. Give Him time, creativity, and trust and watch what He can do!

Sometimes as a parent it's tough for me to evaluate my children's requests. If my daughter asks for a new pair of jeans and needs them, then I will quickly meet that need. However, if she pleads for name-brand jeans to fit a social norm at school, I may or may not get them. I have to assess the harm/benefit of what the underlying issue is. Is this about peer pressure? Significance? Or simply just a good fitting pair of jeans?

In other words, the motives behind the request have a lot to do with my willingness to fulfill the wish. It's the same with God. James 4:3 (NIV) says, "When you ask, you do not receive, because you ask with wrong motives, that you may spend what you get on your pleasures."

We often ask for specific things; a job, a spouse, a child, a home. At times that is precisely what we need, and God supplies. Other times though, God knows there is something more profound than the request, and it's more important to heal the inner hurt. Or frankly, sometimes our desires are 100% selfish, and God's answer is a straightforward "No!"

There is another type of asking my kids do that I think we pray for as well: intercession or intervention. This type of request can run the gamut from, "Mom, will you help me button this shirt?" to, "I can't get this math problem!"

These are the moments' help is needed, a request for instruction or physical support. Just like the case when an object is asked for, as a parent I base my actual intervention on the overall big picture. It is my knowledge of my children and what they need that helps guide what my response will be. When my son was four and needed me to button his shirt, I readily jumped at the asking. When he was five, I asked him to try first, and after some struggle, I interceded. At six, however, it's all him. He needs to figure it out on his own.

That's not me being a cruel parent. It's me knowing his capabilities and nudging him into autonomy on this particular skill.

If you notice, even at an early age, things that take effort for kids are usually balked at. I still remember as a new parent eagerly placing my two-month-old daughter on her stomach for "tummy time," surprised that she cried at the struggle to hold her heavy head up. She didn't ask in words, but her tears and red face communicated a pleading for me to intervene and rescue her from the exercise. I had to deny her desire, for the greater good of muscle development.

When I evaluate what I'm asking God to intercede on something and find an element of rescuing, it should clue me into the fact this may be something that God won't answer, as it will build character or strength to go through. When we ask God to intervene, we must trust that He sees the big picture. He knows whether stepping in will be helpful or will rob us of some unforeseen development essential for our maturity.

Prayer as communication is full of all of the things communication between my children and I have. While I get a lot of requests and a lot of questions and grumbles, I'll tell you what delights me; praise.

It's pretty unusual at this stage in the game to have unprompted gratitude spill out of my kids' mouths, but when it happens, the sweetness of it lasts for days. I'm not talking about the placating thank you, or manipulative kindness to get something in return. I mean the sincere, "Mom, you did a good job on dinner tonight." Or, "Thanks for helping me practice spelling today." The spontaneity of their words is always a little bubble of warmth that bursts inside me. It reminds me how much God relishes our praise. Even simple words of thanksgiving are a sweet aroma of goodness to Him.

There is another part of communication that is essential but extremely hard: repentance. My children seem to have the hardest time saying, "I'm sorry." Despite their ability to eloquently ask for things, or complain in a flourish of drama and expression, when it comes to apologizing the words are often choked on. They mumble these two words in hushed tones, and I watch them try hard to swallow them back down as if it is physically painful to utter them.

However, apologies and confessions must happen. Without the words, invisible walls pop up between us. As their parent, I feel the disconnect and injured relationship when I know they are keeping something from me or are unwilling to say they were in the wrong.

Those two little words bring instant healing. They may fight saying them, but once uttered, I see their bodies relax. They know immediately we are mended, and there is no longer a barrier in our relationship.

The same thing happens in prayer. Psalm 32:5 (NIV) says, "Then I acknowledged my sin to you and did not cover up my iniquity. I said, 'I will confess my transgressions to the Lord.' And you forgave the guilt of my sin." God understands that when we knowingly do something wrong, it separates us from Him. That's what sin is, separation. It's not, however, just the act itself that harms the relationship, it is the shame and guilt we feel that becomes a wall between us.

Just like with my kids, the point of apologizing and putting words to the things that stand between us is for our sake. It takes away our feeling of guilt or the shame we place on ourselves and lets the barrier melt away.

Sometimes I think we are like my children. The words get stuck in our mouths. We want to make excuses for our behavior or blame someone else. When we can find the courage to speak specifically in confession to God, the inward healing is instant.

One final thought on prayer as it relates to parents and children. It is the act of communication and the communication of an idea that matters more than the language itself. What I mean, is that there is no formula for my kids to talk to me. I'm not only listening at 5 PM for instance, and they aren't forced to whisper or have a particular posture for me to pay attention to them. I don't judge the eloquence of their phrases or weigh my response based on how long they've been talking.

We can communicate with God in any way and at any time. Our eyes can be open or closed; we can sit or kneel or stand. We can whisper or scream or sing or just think words. It can be one second or one hour or communication. Prayer is the conduit or channel that connects us to God.

Communication, in the family example, is merely the means by which we grow in understanding of one another, and consequently have our needs addressed and wishes dealt with. It builds our relationship, and the relationship is the framework that creates character and provides my children with the tools to define their purpose. Prayer then can be thought of in the same way. As we communicate with God, we nourish that relationship, understanding more of Him and simultaneously learning more about ourselves. Oswald Chamber says it well as he ends his thoughts on prayer, "Prayer changes *mo,* and then I change things."

Chapter 8 **Blessings**

I am not a shopper. As a teenager, I so rejected the idea of shopping that I have many memories of sitting in our minivan with a book, sweltering in the heat of the day, as my mother and sisters shopped. It wasn't even that I was a bookworm, I just loathed shopping so much that I became a reader to avoid the task.

When you couple my dislike of shopping with my tendency to be frugal you get a slightly bland outdated wardrobe and equally barren living space. I took pride in wearing things decades old and embraced the used clothes, and home furnishings friends passed on in pity. Birthdays and gift-giving holidays were no better, and I would dread the need to buy things for other people. Usually, I resolved the tension of the expectations of others that warred with my loathing of shopping and spending money, by creating artwork for people.

As I matured into adulthood, it became apparent, there were two types of people: gift givers and non-gift givers. You can guess my category.

The most surprising thing happened though when I became a parent. Suddenly, there were these little beings that I loved so deeply and entirely, and I wanted to shower them with things. I found I enjoyed wandering the aisles of a store, looking for something I knew would light up their little faces in delight.

It wasn't just about spending money on them or acquiring items. I found joy in finding ways to bless them.

What changed? Surely, I loved my friends and family, was that not enough to want to spoil them on those holidays of the past? Why was it so hard, before kids, to enjoy gift giving?

I think there are at least two reasons it's different for my children. One, they are dependent on me. At this point in their lives, my husband and I are it. They rely on us for their food, their housing, their clothing, their safety, their well-being, etc. I am inherently aware of that responsibility always. Contrary to what logically makes sense, instead of being a burden, their sole reliance on me increases my desire to bring goodness to them.

The second aspect that makes this different than gifting other friends and family is how well I know my children. I have confidence, in other words, that whatever extra thing I want to provide or surprise them with, will, in fact, be well received.

The more personal the gift or favor, the more powerful it is in blessing that person. For my middle son, whose love language in part at least is food, I know that surprising him with a favorite snack or fixing his favorite meal for supper, will have him beaming. The youngest, however, would be delighted with a box of new markers or coloring book. My daughter, who is a shopper and loves textures and colors and the experience of being in a store, can hardly contain her joy when I offer an hour to take her thrifting.

Each child is incredibly unique in their interests and personalities. As their parent, I know exactly how to make them smile with unexpected joy, and I, myself, relish the opportunities I find to do this.

These two factors of blessing, someone's need and knowing them well, help me understand why I have struggled with gift giving towards others. Either the need isn't there, or I don't know them well enough to know what will be appreciated.

It had to be one of our first Christmases as parents that something clicked. As I found myself eagerly anticipating the morning of gift opening, not for myself, but for seeing how charmed my daughter would be with the gifts it hit me; God himself enjoys blessing us!

Think about it! If I, in my little human way, look for ways and get excited with the idea of knocking the socks off my kids with unexpected things, how much more must God do this? He knows me better than I know myself! He also has unlimited in resources. Combined, that lends itself to some potentially wonderful blessings.

One of the verses that capture this well is Psalm 37:4 (NIV), "Take delight in the Lord, and he will give you the desires of your heart." That's what it feels like I am doing with my kids, finding little ways to fill the unique desires of their hearts. God just does it more perfectly!

Can you think right now of a way God has blessed you? Maybe something unexpected and good that you can give God credit for?

Someone reading this may be scowling just about now. Blessings? Desires? Since when has God blessed me with anything? I would never want to underestimate someone's pain and struggle by implying a rose-tinted existence of gifts and comfortable living.

There are several reasons we may not recognize that God is trying to bless us. One reason may be that our understanding of what a blessing is, is tainted by the words we use and our experience of blessing in our human world. Part of the problem is the similarity we place on blessing and gift in our language.

We've used the words interchangeably because, in our modern day, blessing has come to mean giving or receiving some godly gift. Think about the social media phrase #blessed. People use it to imply they are happy, or enviable, or to have been given much, etc. People say they are #blessed when they go on vacation or get a new car, or after a scholarship or promotion at work. If this is our understanding of blessing in the biblical sense, no wonder some people are looking at their lives bitterly saying, "Why hasn't God Blessed me?"

Perhaps we have the idea of blessing wrong. The Bible has two meanings for the concept of blessing. The actual word, blessing, from the Bible, is *eulogia* or *eulogeo'*. What English word does that remind you of? Eulogy, right? The Greek meaning is from the *eu,* which means good and *logos* which means word. This word we translate as blessing then means "a good word." It's pronouncing a good word over someone. A prayer of thanksgiving then is a blessing. This is where the term for the prayer before a meal comes from. "Who will offer a blessing before we begin?"

There is a second Greek word that we translate as blessed, which is *makarios*. *Makarios* is the Greek word happy. Before you get excited that the Bible promises us happiness, we need to see where the use of this term is. One of the more familiar places to find this word is in the Beatitudes, as in "Blessed are the poor in spirit… blessed are those who mourn…blessed are those who hunger…" (Matthew Chapter 5). This passage seems to oppose our secular understanding of blessing being equal to trips, success, money, health, etc.

Besides often being off on what we think a blessing or gift from God may look like, my interactions as a parent with my children have also opened my eyes to some other reasons we may not notice God's blessings in our lives.

Let me set this up. The delight I mentioned earlier that I feel as I look for ways to bring happiness to my kids, is independent of their experience. In other words, I can feel warm fuzzies inwardly as I plan a random act of kindness for my kids, but their ability to feel blessed is up to them. One time I decided to surprise my kids over a school break. There is a place about an hour's drive from our home where you can dig for crystals. They've had friends bring back cool treasures from this site and have requested many times that we go. The night before the surprise trek, I researched the place and felt the excitement as I planned out our journey and what other fun stops we'd make along the way. The next morning as I eagerly announced the day's adventure, all I heard were moans and grumbles. Although I had fun working out a plan to bless them, they couldn't receive it. Their whines and protests didn't change the gift itself, but they missed the experience of it as a present.

Unfortunately, as a parent, these times when the happiness felt on my end is disproportionate to what my children end up feeling are common. What gets in the way, then, of their ability to soak up goodness? I will tell you, entitlement and self-reliance.

When my kids tend to have something frequently, it seeps into them and begins to shift their expectations to a right or necessity. There is a particular brand of cereal they love, that I can only get at one store. When I make that effort over and over again, they begin to overlook the blessing and presume it will always be there. While the cereal is still a blessing, and it's still an act of goodness that I am bestowing on them, their entitlement interferes with their ability to appreciate it.

I know I do the same thing with God. Whenever my husband and I have moved into a new home, those first weeks going to bed, I am usually overwhelmed in gratitude to God. I find myself grateful for a roof, and bed, and electricity. I'm often spouting off thanksgivings, that everything fell into place with the mortgage, that we were able to sell our old home, that we got everything moved. My cup as they say, is usually overflowing as I am aware of God's blessing. The house we live in now, we've been in 7 years. I am struck writing this that I've let that recognition of God's favor seep away. In the consistency of having a home, I have lost sight that it is a gift to be able to live here.

70

Let's look at James 1:17 (NIV) which says, "Every good and perfect gift is from above, coming down from the Father of the heavenly lights, who does not change like shifting shadows." James here talks about good gifts. What do you think of when you hear the word good? This word comes from the Greek word *agathos* which means useful, intrinsically good, pleasant, joyful, upright, honorable, kind, convenient, or riches. That is a pretty broad definition of good! I can fit so many things that occur in my day or look around at what is before me this moment and call them good. Which means I am being bombarded by gifts from God every moment of every day, I just don't stop to see them, or I wrongfully take credit for them.

The other way my children miss out on my blessings is through their independence. It's hard for me to surprise them with a favorite meal if they help themselves to a hotdog and chips before dinner is ready. Self-reliance isn't necessarily a terrible thing until we take care of so many things in our strength that we leave little room for God to provide.

Let's say you've gotten yourself in a bind with your schedule, and maybe you are even ill, or someone in your family is, and a friend says, "Let me help, what can I do?" If you pull up your martyr pants and declare you are okay, patting yourself on the back for your ability to take care of everything, then don't be surprised to find yourself experiencing a lack of blessings. Not because God isn't trying to shower you with goodness, but because you keep saying no thank you, I've got this.

One last thought before we wrap this up. All this talk of blessings and gifts may have you wondering, can you earn these things? When I say earned, I mean, can we deservedly gain blessings or gifts based on our behavior or achievements? The New Testament translates the word "gift" from the Greek words *doron* or *dorea*. In the definitions of these words, you will find emphasized that these are freely given and not acquired by merit.

Do blessings or gifts come from merit then? Well, for your child's birthday, would your gift for them change based on how many chores they did around the house? Would you give one child more gifts for Christmas because they got in trouble less than one of your other children?

There is a word for honoring someone's achievements or efforts, and that word is reward. It is most often used in the Bible when speaking of the end of time but is never with phrases containing blessing or gift.

Being a parent has taught me how fun it is to bring pleasure to my kids. I actively seek ways to surprise them and increase their joy. It is because I know them so well, their likes and dislikes, and because I know they rely on me for the essentials, that I find it so satisfying to bless them. Their ability to receive that blessing is another matter altogether. If they are spoiled and expectant or too self-reliant, it makes it hard for them to experience the joy of unexpected favor.

God is eternally looking for ways to bless me. Matthew 7:11(NIV) says, "If you, then, though you are evil, know how to give good gifts to your children, how much more will your Father in heaven give good gifts to those who ask him!" He wants to make me smile, to have me be in awe of how perfect his gifts are for me, but as with my kids, it's up to me on how I will encounter and accept those blessings.

Chapter 9 **Selfishness**

It's fascinating to me how innately selfish children are. You can observe this at very young ages. With my first child, I can recall watching her at just 18 months of age, yanking toys out of other kid's hands. Of course, the toy theft was often reciprocated by other children as well, but the first time it happened publicly I was mortified. By the time my third one came around, I was parent-wise, and knew this was just part of normal toddler development.

Now that my children are past the grab and hold stage, I can find it amusing to watch a group of toddlers fight over a toy. If you don't have kids and have been horrified when you see this type of selfish behavior, have no fear, the behavior part of that extreme possessiveness does fade.

The word uttered by children that perfectly communicates this self-centered stance on life is none other than, "Mine!" This word was certainly a part of some of those first 20-30 words each of my kids learned. As they have aged, they learned to socially not steal toys or scream "Mine!", but this hasn't dampened their natural selfishness or what they are saying on the inside.

How do I know this? My children aren't ashamed to request the largest amount of dessert or keep track to the second on how much screen time the other sibling is allowed. They gift count at Christmas and lick count cake battered beaters. Their obsessiveness over fairness is nothing more than self-centeredness, disguised as justice. When they say, "That's not fair," they are saying, "I deserve more."

Witnessing my children's greed has taught me a lot about my selfishness, and ultimately since we are discussing theological topics, how selfishness ties into sin.

I would have to say that the most startling revelation, as a parent, is that maturing into adulthood doesn't magically eliminate self-centeredness. More likely, aging just teaches us how to mask it better.

When there is one cookie left, and two of my children hover to ensure I split it perfectly, still both complaining that the other got more, it's because we are in our own home. If we were at a friend's house, my children have learned socially not to be so dramatic and selfish. Does that change their innate desire to have the most? Absolutely not! I know this because back in the safety of our home, the complaining of fairness and who got more or less at the friend's house starts up again.

But let's be honest here, am I much different? How many times have I envied someone else's massive piece of chocolate silk pie, but swallowed down my discontent to hide my inner selfish nature? It's hard to admit, but I've even kept track of how many cookies my husband has after a meal to make sure I get to enjoy the same amount.

When I take my kids out shopping, and they beg to buy a toy and moan loudly when I tell them they don't need more toys, I can't be too hard on them, when I find myself inwardly craving something on another aisle. Just because I don't have the money to buy everything I want, doesn't mean I don't have the same response as my kids do to toys. I've just learned not to verbalize it.

So, what does this have to do with faith? Everything!

First, let's understand what selfishness is. Merriam-Webster defines it as being, "concerned excessively or exclusively with oneself." In other words, placing yourself as priority number one.

Emphasizing your needs and wants over others is the exact opposite of what Christianity preaches. In fact, it's the antithesis of the great commandment. Recall that in the book of Matthew someone asks Christ which the greatest commandment in the Law is. Verses 37-39 of Matthew chapter 22 (NIV) says, "Jesus replied: 'Love the Lord your God with all your heart and with all your soul and with all your mind.' This is the first and greatest commandment. And the second is like it: 'Love your neighbor as yourself.'"

Christ says God should be priority one, second is your neighbor, which leaves yourself at most as the third priority.

In kids, It's easy to see when they put themselves excessively first, but it can be much trickier with adults. There are many good virtues that society finds acceptable but are still selfish. Happiness is one example. A secular society would say this is something we should pursue wholeheartedly and sometimes even exclusively. Happiness is not a sin, however, could you see how the pursuit of happiness could become selfish, and ultimately a sin?

Let's go all the way back to The Fall, recorded in Genesis as the first sin, and the choice that sets our future in motion as we know it. Eating the forbidden fruit is the quintessential decision that separated us from God, and if we examine it, we will find this first sin is that of selfishness.

In Genesis Chapter 3, the serpent uses his craftiness to entice Eve to sin by eating the forbidden fruit. He tells Eve in verse 5, "For God knows that when you eat from it your eyes will be opened, and you will be like God, knowing good and evil."

When Eve chose to eat the fruit, the sin wasn't just about breaking a rule. It was the decision of man to put himself on equal terms with God. Adam and Eve weren't just hungry; they had plenty of other food. They wanted to be Gods.

If you move through the Bible, at the heart of every sin, you will find selfishness. Let's just go to the very next sin recorded in Genesis chapter 4. Here is the story of two brothers, Cain and Abel who bring an offering to God. Abel is unselfish and delivers the best portions to God, Cain is selfish and saves the best for himself. God wasn't pleased with Cain, and in a fit of selfish jealousy, Cain kills his brother.

It is no wonder then why God is trying to rescue us from sin. If behind every sin, is the decision to choose ourselves above either God or someone else, then it stands to reason that this selfishness turns us away from God. If we pick ourselves, we deny God.

Still unsure? Let's check in with the Ten Commandments. The first four commandments are essentially saying, God is to be number one, so be unselfish; No other Gods, no graven images, no misusing His name and keep His day holy. The next six specifically speak of things relating to selfish behavior; dishonoring parents, killing, adultery, stealing, lying, and coveting. The battle between self and God as boss of our actions and motivations is behind all sin.

The New Testament is no different. You will find at the heart of everything the conflict of self versus Christ.   In fact, Jesus says in three of the gospels that being unselfish is how you become a disciple.   Luke 9:23 says it this way in the New Living Translation, "Then he said to the crowd, "If any of you wants to be my follower, you must turn from your selfish ways, take up your cross daily, and follow me."

Why does the Bible harp on this? What harm does selfishness do? James 3:16 (NIV) says, "For where you have envy and selfish ambition, there you find disorder and every evil practice." The Greek word in this verse for disorder is *akatastasia* which means literally cannot stand. The definition includes instability, unsettled, tumult, and confusion. Selfishness leads to instability. It causes chaos and confusion.

I can definitely say that my children's selfish outbursts have led to tumult and disorder. Here's something else parenting has taught me; we come into this world selfish. In fact, the draw to selfishness is always present. Left to themselves, without any correction or input from society, my children would consistently seek to please themselves first, and others second. I have watched my children become publicly less selfish, but their self-seeking nature is still quite strong, just as mine is!

What raising children have convinced me of, is that Christ alone can bend our will towards unselfishness. Just setting up rules and having lectures about helping others and encouraging humility may change behavior but not necessarily change character.

Paul, the great Biblical missionary, speaks quite eloquently about all of this in Romans. He calls selfishness being controlled by the flesh. He says it like this, "We know that the law is spiritual; but I am unspiritual, sold as a slave to sin. I do not understand what I do. For what I want to do I do not, but what I hate I do." Romans 7:14-15 (NIV).

Paul, who of anyone, knew right from wrong, says that he can't seem to do the right thing. His selfish side keeps winning out. I see this in my kid's lives every day and unfortunately at least inwardly in myself just as often.

I don't' know about you, but I find this is disheartening. The pull within me to place myself first is powerful. What then is the solution? The Spirit. Paul addresses his dilemma in the description of selfishness and godliness in Chapter 8 of Romans, verse 5, "Those who live according to the flesh have their minds set on what their flesh desires; but those who live in accordance with the Spirit have their minds set on what the Spirit desires."

The Spirit he refers to is the Holy Spirit which dwells within us. The Holy Spirit is a gift to those who believe (Acts 2:38). It is the job of the Holy Spirit to teach and help us (John 14:26). Most importantly, the things that the Spirit desires would be unselfish things, or as Paul outlines in the book of Galatians, the fruits of the Spirit. Galatians 5:22-23 (NIV) says, "But the fruit of the Spirit is love, joy, peace, patience, kindness, goodness, faithfulness, gentleness, and self-control." Are not all those qualities a part of someone we would consider genuinely unselfish?!

Every time we put ourselves at the center, we displace God. Children don't grasp that concept yet, but we should. C.S. Lewis says in his book The Problem of Pain that choosing ourselves as the center, "...is the fall in every individual life, and in each day of each individual life, the basic sin behind all particular sins: at this very moment you and I are either committing it, or about to commit it, or repenting it.

As we age, our natural selfishness doesn't necessarily dwindle away; we just learn to hide it in more socially acceptable ways. Perhaps then, as we watch and witness children's innate tendency towards selfishness, we should consider it a blessing. It can remind us to be aware of our inward thoughts and desires.

I crave the day my selfish nature is truly dead, though my guess is that won't be until my outward flesh is gone. Until then I will ask daily, if not moment by moment, for the Holy Spirit to work in and refine me.

Chapter 10 **Grace**

We've covered quite a few theological topics that can stir up questions within ourselves, within our faith community, and within a secular world. Many religions have been born to answer these questions of pain, autonomy, judgment, blessings, and hope. Other world faiths teach beliefs that at times mimic truths in Christianity, and at other times seem to contradict. But, if you had to pick out the one thing about Christianity that makes it unique to all other religions, it would be grace.

What all the major world religions set out to do, through their existence, is to help humanity become better versions of themselves. All of them have an endpoint or a destination, and though the names of this endpoint differ, at the core the end game in all faiths is about righteousness.

Righteousness. Let's be honest, who is ready to call it a day on reading now that this outdated word has come up? We don't talk a lot in our daily conversations about righteousness, so first, we need to understand what the word means. At its center, righteousness is fulfilling the standard of what is right and good. I don't know about you, but when I hear the word righteousness, I automatically have this visual of a giant magnifying glass coming out of the sky to start finding all of my flaws, which makes me want to run away!

To be able to understand how differently Christianity handles the answer to being righteous, we need to look at how the other major religions view righteousness.

For Buddhists following the Noble Eightfold Path earns you righteousness, or the ability to end suffering and live in complete peace. The emphasis is having a right view, right resolve, right speech, right conduct, right livelihood, right effort, right mindfulness, and right meditation.

Hindus also follow a path to righteousness, and Dharma, as they call it, is achieved by living one's life according to the codes and conduct described in the Hindu scriptures. The ten essential rules for observing Dharma are patience, forgiveness, self-control, honesty, sanctity, control of senses, reason, learning, truthfulness, and absence of anger.

A Muslim is considered righteous when they submit completely to Allah's will. Obedience to Allah's commands and acting on whatever he legislates is what makes you righteous and gains you prosperity in this world and the next. The Five Pillars of Islam, which are considered mandatory, are faith, prayer, charity, fasting, and pilgrimage to Mecca.

We are familiar, from studying the Old Testament, what the Jews deem as righteousness, which is both being a part of God's covenant as well as keeping the law that the covenant outlined. As long as the Jews uphold the Torah, they are considered righteous. The Torah is the five books of Moses: Genesis, Exodus, Leviticus, Numbers, and Deuteronomy.

Christianity is no different in regard to speaking about and advocating for righteousness. The significant distinction is in how to achieve that righteousness. In all of the other world religions, the responsibility resides in you. You must do the right thing, which as outlined above, differs based on what religion you follow.

Christianity alone takes the responsibility off of you. 2 Corinthians 5:21 (NIV) states this, "God made him who had no sin to be sin for us, so that in him we might become the righteousness of God." Did you catch that? Christ is our righteousness. He followed all of the law, the right paths, was obedient, etc. He was the ultimate righteous person, and then he let his life stand in the place of our inability to ever live a perfect life.

Here is where our conversation turns from righteousness to grace. The distinction between all of the other world religions and Christianity is even more significant than the idea that someone else did the hard work of achieving righteousness for us. That is incredible in and of itself, but what the concept of grace explains is that Christ did that without expecting any repayment. Grace defined is undeserved favor. He took your place, even though you didn't deserve the gift, and demands nothing in return except acknowledgment and acceptance of the gift.

In our society, we live by retributive, distributive, and procedural justice. Each of these types of justice is different, but all are concerned with fairness. Retributive justice says people get what they deserve. Distributive justice is economically making sure everyone gets their fair share. Procedural justice is making decisions according to fair treatment. Grace stands in conflict with these forms of justice because first and foremost grace isn't fair.

Because grace isn't natural in a justice-oriented society, it can be tough to comprehend. Thus, when we hear about God's grace offered to us, usually, we find ourselves tipping to one of two extremes. Some of us secretly think we do deserve grace (we are worthy), and some of us secretly cannot believe we deserve grace (we are unworthy). I'm hoping that as we look at parents and children, we can more fully understand what it is to experience and embrace grace.

Since the definition of grace is undeserved favor, we need to look no further than at young children to see grace in action. In their infancy, children can do very little for themselves. In their helpless state, they cannot do anything to earn the right to be fed, held, and cleaned. When I would wake at 2 AM to feed my daughter, it wasn't because I had kept track of her behavior during the day and decided she deserved it. I woke and fed her because I loved her and wanted what was best for her, which at that moment was to have her tummy filled. Some may say it was my duty, that's why I fed my daughter. True, it was my responsibility, but had it been only a chore, it would have looked much different. Likely if it were just an item to cross off, with no relational aspect, I would have groaned and even complained audibly to her for waking me up. I would not have been very gentle and may not have held her, but just have propped up a bottle.

I remember very distinctly sitting on my couch holding my daughter when she was six days old and examining every minute detail of her face. As I sat there, I thought to myself, I would do absolutely anything for this child, yet she has done nothing to earn that response from me, except merely exist. It was the first time I realized what love without condition was; favor unearned.

I grant grace to my children daily. That trend of feeding my children continues. I still feed them every day, even when they scrunch up their noses and say, "What is this?" in disgusted tones. I drive them to school and events, supply them with clothes to wear. They have a home, and a place to sleep, despite not contributing economically to any of this.

When my son was in first grade, the fad was pedometers. Over the Christmas holiday, it seemed half of his class were sporting some variety of step-counter and challenging each other in competition. My son wanted to participate, but I told him he'd have to pay for one himself. I searched online and found an inexpensive step-counter for $10. He did some odd jobs and saved up and finally bought it. His excitement was palpable the first day he took it to school. It had a clip to secure it to your clothes, but my son was insistent he wanted it in his pocket. You can guess where this is heading. That very first night of owning a pedometer, he lost it somewhere outside of our home. He was devastated, and the tears he cried that night were heavy.

My husband and I could have gone the route of giving him what he deserved. We easily could have used it as a teaching moment, and encouraged him to save up again, and be more careful with his belongings the next time. Instead, we opted for a different lesson; grace. We even used those words, "We want to give you grace. Despite not deserving it, we are going to get you a replacement."

My kids do the wrong thing quite often. They fight with each other. They're caught lying. They leave huge messes. They break things. They argue and resist work. If I based my affection and response outwardly to them on their behavior, they'd be miserable, because they would get little from me.

My love for them though is unconditional. I treat them not as they deserve, but with grace. You may be fortunate to have had an abundance of this type of love in your life. Typically, though, the kind of love we encounter is conditional. The more we've experienced conditional love, the harder it is to accept pure unconditional love.

I asked my family once if they had just one thing they wish they would have understood or known about earlier in life, what it would be. Without hesitation, though said in different ways, each person talked about wishing they had grasped the concept of grace earlier. The best way for me to think of it is this; there is nothing I can do, to make God love me more and there is nothing I can do, to make God love me less. I feel this wholeheartedly with my children, and God feels this wholeheartedly for you and me.

And here is what is incredible, God's scale for grace is infinitely more than mine is as a parent. While it may help to think about grace in the way parents love and provide for children despite their children's deservedness and behavior, God's perfect grace is far more lavish.

I use an allegory to help me grasp it. Let's say you committed a crime, an intentional nasty crime. You were rightfully accused, and the punishment for your crime was death. You sat in your prison cell awaiting the date. There also was a Noble at this time with vast amounts of wealth and power. He had one heir, whom he loved very much, who was set to take over the business and inherit everything one day. The morning of the execution came. You sat in your cell in anticipation, when suddenly the jailer appeared with the Noble's son. "I'm here to take your place," said the son. With that, someone opened the cell door and set you free, while the heir was locked up to die for your crime. Ready to weep at your redemption as you stepped out into freedom, there was a hand on your shoulder. The jailer was there with more news. "The nobleman has asked for you, as you are to be the new heir. All he has is now yours."

The book of Galatians talks about this, first in Gal 3:13 we read, "But Christ has rescued us from the curse pronounced by the law. When he was hung on the cross, he took upon himself the curse for our wrongdoing." (NLT) and then later in Gal 4:5, "God sent him to buy freedom for us who were slaves to the law, so that he could adopt us as his very own children." (NLT)

Grace isn't just avoiding punishment; it is elaborate love. Christ didn't come just to redeem but to restore as well. With our children, we experience grace not only by letting them off the hook when they deserve a consequence but also by providing them with more than they expect.

The story of the prodigal son is one of the ways Jesus tried to teach us about grace. You can read the whole story in Luke chapter

15. In essence, it is a story of a son who squandered his father's wealth and came back home expecting to be made a servant. His father did the unexpected and welcomed him back not as a servant but as a son. That his father even agreed to let him back home was the redemption part, but grace provided restoration as well, and he was welcomed as a son and heir once again.

In the parable Jesus told, one of the striking things he mentions is the fact that the father, once seeing his lost son in the distance, goes running to him. Running to greet someone was unheard of in that culture and symbolized how eager and extravagant the father's love was. It reminds me that grace is often entwined with hope. Hope as we discussed in an earlier chapter comes before action, and grace, in this case, is the response.

If we can think about how we raise children with unconditional love that doesn't force them to earn every aspect of affection and caregiving, maybe it can help us understand how God loves us. There is nothing my children can do to make me love them more and nothing they can do to make me love them less. I do not base my love on their merit. My love started at conception, and I expect it will never end.

STUDY QUESTIONS

Pain & Suffering Questions

1. Have you met people who have left their religion/church/faith? What reasons do they give?

2. What painful or trying things have you experienced as a result of just living in our world as it is? (I.E. nature, weather, how you were born, sibling order, the family you were born into)

3. Read Romans 8:20 (NIV) "For the creation was subjected to frustration, not by its own choice, but by the will of the one who subjected it, in hope...". Any ideas what this is saying?
   a. The word "frustration" is the Greek work *mataiotes*, which means aimlessness, not having any purpose or meaning. In other words, creation itself has been affected by sin. Creation lost its purpose because of man. In fact, it is a "slave", but to what? Look at verse 21. It says it will be set free from decay, which is rottenness and destruction.
   b. What is some evidence you see of creation in decay?

4. If we don't like the idea that the world/environment just naturally occurs, then the alternative is that things happen to us based on merit/worthiness or the strength of our prayers. Read Matthew 5:45 (NIV) "He causes his sun to rise on the evil and the good, and sends rain on the righteous and the unrighteous." How does this scripture refute the idea that we have something to do with the weather?

5. Think of an inadvertent annoyance/pain/emotional hurt you experienced this month because of another human being.

6. Now think of a deliberate one. Does one hurt more, or does it depend?

7. Can you think of any examples of self-inflicted pain? (Suffering from choices we make)

8. Look up Exodus 20. Write down the ten commandments. It's easy to see how breaking the last six can cause personal suffering. But look at the first four – how does breaking each of those cause personal suffering?

9. What are other things the Bible instructs us to do or not do, that can save us from future pain if we abide by the wisdom?

10. If you could choose would you rather 1) keep you child from ever experiencing any pain or negativity, knowing that it would mean your child would need to always live with you, be dependent on you, and never enter "the world")? Or would you choose 2) allow your child to become an independent individual guaranteed to experience pain and difficulty, but with the potential to use that to grow and contribute to other?

Trust Questions

1. If you are a parent, what are some of the surprises, both good and bad, that you experienced once you had children?

2. Read Mark 10:15 (NIV). "Truly I tell you, anyone who will not receive the Kingdom of God like a little child will never enter it."
   a. How do children usually receive gifts?

3. Do you have any kids in your life that are risk takers? Does it affect how easy it is to trust you?

4. How have you seen experience specifically cause you, a child, or someone you know, to be slow to trust?

5. Would you consider yourself someone who trusts easily and quickly, or someone who is cautious and skeptical initially?

6. Can you think of a time what you were irritated that a child wouldn't trust your encouragement to do or try something? Why was that irritating?

7. The Greek word used for faith or trust is *pistis*. Interestingly it comes from the Greek word *peitho* which means to persuade or be persuaded. What does it take to be persuaded to do something out of your comfort zone?

8. Is there anything you know God has asked you to trust him on, that you are hesitating with?

9. Who is someone in your life who you would say seems to display a supernatural trust In God almost always? Does this person have stories of God's faithfulness in the past?

Discipline Questions

1. How would you describe your discipline style? Is it different from spouse/in-laws/parents?

2. What are the differences between discipline, abuse, and punishment?

3. What comes easier to you, giving external consequences or allowing natural consequences?

4. Can you think of some examples of lax discipline that leads to worsening behavior within your family or close friends?

5. Why don't we like the idea of a God who disciplines?

6. What are some specific character traits you think God is working on in you? Can you think of signs of his "discipline"?

7. Do you have different personalities in your home that allow for different ways of discipline? If so, give some examples.

8. Read Isaiah 28:24-29 (NIV):
"When a farmer plows for planting, does he plow continually?
Does he keep on breaking up and working the soil?
25When he has leveled the surface,
does he not sow caraway and scatter cumin?
Does he not plant wheat in its place, barley in its plot, and spelt in its field?
26His God instructs him and teaches him the right way.
27Caraway is not threshed with a sledge, nor is the wheel of a cart rolled over cumin; caraway is beaten out with a rod, and cumin with a stick.

28Grain must be ground to make bread; so one does not go on threshing it forever. The wheels of a threshing cart may be rolled over it, but one does not use horses to grind grain.
29All this also comes from the Lord Almighty, whose plan is wonderful, whose wisdom is magnificent."

Notice verse 26 uses the word instruct. In Hebrew this is the word for discipline. What is this verse implying about discipline and instruction?

9. Can you think of a time God may have needed to escalate his guidance to get your attention? Share that if you can.

Free Will Questions

1. What are some things you wish you had complete control over with your kids?

2. Is there anything about the idea of free will that bothers you? If so, what is it?

3. What would be some benefits and harms of being surrounded only by things and beings that were not autonomous (no free will or ability to make decisions)?

4. Do your children, your spouse, or friends do and choose things that are very predictable? Give some examples?

5. What are some unique boundaries you have in place in your home, that come from your own issues or specific issues based on the personality of one of your kids?

6. Can you think of a situation where you hoped someone would make a good decision, despite knowing they probably wouldn't?

7. What is the very first example of free will in the Bible? (Look up Genesis 2:16)

8. Do you think God was surprised by "The Fall" with Adam and Eve? Explain.

9. Read Genesis 3:24 (NIV)
   "After he drove the man out, he placed on the east side of the Garden of Eden Cherubim and a flaming sword flashing back and forth to guard the way to the tree of life."
   What is preventing man from eternal life now?
   This foreshadows that blood would be required to get back to wholeness and right relationship with God. Did you ever think

that God already had a plan to reconcile us with Jesus's blood even at the moment of the Fall?

Hope & Disappointment Questions

1. Think of two examples of something you hope for and something you wish for. Now think about what percentage point of probability you'd put on either one happening. Is there a difference for hope vs wish?

2. Name some specific hopes you have for your children, or other children in your life.

3. Have you seen people that put their own personal hopes *onto* their kids? What are some examples?

4. What is something you have had to persevere for or through? How does hope effect your ability to persevere?

5. On a scale of 1 -10 (1 being not at all, 10 being the most extreme), how much does it bother you to think about disappointing someone?

6. Have you ever felt that God must be disappointed in you?

7. Do you think God is ever surprised?

8. Read Romans 8:28 (NIV)

   "And we know that in all things God works for the good of those who love him, who have been called according to his purpose."

   The Greek word used here for good is *agathos* which means good as in essential goodness, or good in nature, kind, generous. Think opposite of evil. If you had to choose, do you think God is aiming for good character (internal) or good circumstances (external)?

9. God is using all of our circumstances and choices (bad and good) to build us into better humans not to give us better things. How does internalizing that truth change your perspective on the future? Does this give you hope?

10. What are some things you think God is hoping for, for you?

Judgement Questions

1. Have you ever heard people complain that Christians are too judgmental? What issue has that statement surrounded?

2. Picture one of the more judgmental people you know, and one of the least judgmental people you know. Besides the issue of judgment, what are other big differences in those individuals lives?

3. How would you explain the difference between making a judgment and differentiating about a behavior as being right or wrong?

4. The words discriminate, differentiate, or make a distinction, all mean the same thing. But do these words carry different meaning socially? Why is that?

5. Have you been around a child that has embarrassed you with some judgmental statement? Tell about it.

6. Do you think kids naturally grade behavior as right or wrong, or is that taught from our focus on right and wrong?

7. Have you ever tried to justify something you knew was wrong, by finding someone whose behavior was even more wrong than yours?

8. How does our understanding of the true unconditional nature of God's love effect our experience with judgement?

9. Read Matthew 7:3-4 (NIV).

   "Why do you look at the speck of sawdust in your brother's eye and pay no attention to the plank in your own eye? How can you say to your brother, 'Let me take the speck out of your eye,' when all the time there is a plank in your own eye?

Why is it so much easier to see other people's "specks" and miss the planks in our lives?

10. Have you judged someone harshly, only later to hear the whole story and realize you were wrong? Share it if you want.

11. Knowing now what judgment is, how should Christians react socially to immoral behaviors?

Amy Clarkson MD

Prayer Questions

1. What are some questions kids have stumped you on before?

2. Why do you find it hard to pray?

3. Read Matthew 7:11 (NIV)
   "If you, then, though you are evil, know how to give good gifts to your children, how much more will your Father in heaven give good gifts to those who ask him!"

   What are some good gifts you've had fun giving your kids or you remember getting when you were a kid?

4. What is something your children, or you as a child, asked for that was impractical or a bit ridiculous?

5. Read James 4:3 (NIV)
   "When you ask, you do not receive, because you ask with wrong motives, that you may spend what you get on your pleasures."

   What's an example of something you've prayed for that in truth was for the wrong motive?

6. Can you think of anything you intervened in when your kids asked for help that actually delayed independence?

7. Read Luke 11:5-10 (NIV)
   " Then Jesus said to them, "Suppose you have a friend, and you go to him at midnight and say, 'Friend, lend me three loaves of bread; a friend of mine on a journey has come to me, and I have no food to offer him.' And suppose the one inside answers, 'Don't bother me. The door is already locked, and my children and I are in bed. I can't get up and give you anything.'

I tell you, even though he will not get up and give you the bread because of friendship, yet because of your shameless audacity he will surely get up and give you as much as you need.
So I say to you: Ask and it will be given to you; seek and you will find; knock and the door will be opened to you. For everyone who asks receives; the one who seeks finds; and to the one who knocks, the door will be opened."

Paraphrase what happened in this parable.
The parable seems to imply that persistence is important to our requests. Is it for you to ignore the pleads of your children who are persistent, even when you know they don't need what they are asking for?

8. If we sometimes give in to persistent pleas, do you think God sometimes "gives in" to our prayers?
    a. Read 1 Samuel 8 — in Vs 6 what do the Israelites ask for?
    b. In Vs 7 — who is supposed to be their king?
    c. Did God want to give them a King? Vs 9 sounds like a parent warning — "look, it's not going to be good"
    d. Samuel then spends 8 verses telling the Israelites how terrible serving an earthly King would be. What is the Israelites response? (Vs 19)
    e. Just to be clear, what were their motives for wanting a King? (Vs 20).
    f. Despite what God knew would be BEST what does God do? (Vs 22)

9. Do you find it easy to offer spontaneous praise to God? What usually causes you to give thanks to Him?

10. Does confession come easily or is it a challenge? What types of things are easy to say 'I'm sorry' about? What things are hard to say 'I'm sorry' about?

Blessings Questions

1. Tell about some ways you actively seek to bless you kids? OR were blessed by a parent or an adult when you were a kid?

2. Are you a gift giver? If so, what do you like about giving gifts? If not, what is hard about giving gifts?

3. What is an example of something unexpected that you credit God for providing in your life?

4. Have you seen entitlement or self-reliance get in the way of your ability to bless your kids or others in your life?

5. What is something that at the beginning, you thanked God for often, that you've forgotten to thank Him for lately?

6. Read James 1:17 (NIV)
"Every good and perfect gift is from above, coming down from the Father of the heavenly lights, who does not change like shifting shadows."
That word good in Greek is *agathos*. What is your definition of good? The Greek word good means many things— useful, intrinsically good, pleasant, joyful, upright, honorable, kind, convenient, riches. Think of the broadest sense of the word good. Does that match your definition of good?

7. Have you ever taken credit for good things in your life? Give an example. How does this rob God from praise?

8. Can you earn a gift?
There are a few words that we have translated as "gift" that are used in the New Testament. They are the Greek words *doron and dorea.* In the definitions of these words, you will find emphasized that these are freely given and not acquired by merit. Let's see if this pans out.

100

    a. For your child's birthday, would your gift for them change based on how many chores they did around the house?

    b. Would you give one child more gifts for Christmas because they got in trouble less than one of your other children?

10. How does society confuse #blessing with the idea of gifts? Are they the same?

11. Read 1 Peter 3:9 (NIV)
"Do not repay evil with evil or insult with insult. On the contrary, repay evil with blessing, because to this you were called so that you may inherit a blessing."

Does this mean when you are kind you will prosper or have good fortune? Perhaps, but this verse is using the word 'blessing' from *eulogeo,* indicating a good word will be spoken about you. Rephrase this verse, inserting the idea of a good word being spoken for blessing.

9. Read Matthew Chapter 5, *The* Beatitudes. You'll see the word 'blessed' multiple times. This is the Greek word that we translate as blessed, which is *makarios. Makarios* is from the Greek word happy. Do the Beatitudes promise gifts or something different?

10. Let's go back to the question then, in the Bible, is a blessing the same as a gift?

11. If the Bible's use of blessings isn't always the same as our idea of gifts, does that mean God doesn't give gifts?

12. Name some gifts we are promised in the Bible. (I.E. Acts 2:38, Romans 5:17, ETC)

Selfishness Questions

1. Have you seen selfish behavior in toddlers? Does it amuse you or horrify you?

2. Is selfishness as a child necessary? Explain.

3. What is something that you may selfishly want or care about in a public space, that you would never let on outwardly?

4. Read James 3:16 (NIV)
   "For where you have envy and selfish ambition, there you find disorder and every evil practice."

   Name some ramifications you see day to day in your community and nationally that are the result of selfishness.

5. Can you think of some things that are socially acceptable, but at their core are still selfish?

6. C.S. Lewis says that choosing self (or selfishness) is "the basic sin behind all particular sins". Do you agree or disagree with this? Explain.

7. Read Romans 7:14-15 (NIV)
   "We know that the law is spiritual; but I am unspiritual, sold as a slave to sin. I do not understand what I do. For what I want to do I do not, but what I hate I do."
   Does it surprise you to hear these words coming from Paul? Can you relate to this passage? How so?

8. Read Acts 2:38, John 14:26, and Galatians 5:22-23. What do these verses promise about the Holy Spirit?

9. What is an example or evidence in your life of a way the Holy Spirit is working on you? Can you relate that example to selfishness?

Grace Questions

1. What comes to mind when you hear the word righteousness?

2. Why do you think so many religions care about righteousness?

3. What are the differences between grace and fairness? What about justice and mercy?

4. When you think about grace, do you find it easier to identify with the idea that the God of the universe loves YOU and thinks you are AMAZING? Or is it easier to identify with the idea that you are a sinner and can't fathom being worthy enough for Christ to die for?

5. Do you have a memory of realizing there was someone (child, spouse, friend, stranger), that you would literally do anything for, despite them not doing anything to earn that favor?

6. Can you think of someone in your life who's love, or approval seems conditional? How does that contrast to someone in your life who's approval in unconditional?

7. Have you noticed that often the story of salvation often stops with redemption (free of consequence) and doesn't move on to restoration (relationship)? Why is that?

8. What might your life look like (good or bad) if everything that happened to you was based on deservedness?

9. Think about this statement, "There is nothing I can do, to make God love me more and nothing I can do, to make God love me less." Which part of that statement do you have a harder time living out?

Made in the USA
San Bernardino, CA
15 August 2019